D0364642

# Woman's World Cookbook

# South African Favourite Recipes

Selected & edited by Isabel Jones
Photographs by Roger Bell

*Chameleon Press*

# Contents

*Acknowledgements*
Grateful thanks go to the following:
Lesley Faull and the Silwood Kitchen for the use of their gracious premises
for cooking, judging and photography; Alicia Wilkinson, Louise Faull, Lee
Barty and Nikki Black of Silwood Kitchen for their untiring and cheerful
supervision; the Silwood Kitchen student team for their hard work, skill and
enthusiasm; Chris Milne and Esmé Garlick of Woolworths for their highly
professional assistance with the photographic styling; Denise Hull of Vitria
Glassware for the loan of superb glassware for the photographs; Frank
Harrison of Harrison Agencies for the loan of Gray ceramics and GC ware
for the cooking and judging; Hym Rabinowitz for the kind loan of selected
pottery from his studio; Woolworths, Mrs L Faull, Lee Barty, Isabel Jones,
Chris Milne, Ian and Patricia Milne, Marilyn Verster and Sarah Christie for
the loan of props for the photographs; Christopher Peter and the Irma Stern
Museum for fresh herbs from the museum garden.

The recipes in this book have been tested and edited by Woolworths, Afrexco,
Isabel Jones and Lynne Bryer. Thanks go to Woolworths and Janet Hacking,
and (in the case of the venison recipes) to Afrexco, for their expert advice and
suggestions.

Published 1989 by Chameleon Press
19 Estmil Road, Diep River 7800
(Postal: Box 117, Plumstead 7800)
All rights reserved
Text © SABC 1989
Photographs © Roger Bell 1989
Design & Typography: Linda Vicquery
Photographs styled by Isabel Jones
Setting & Reproduction: Unifoto
Printed & Bound by CTP Book Printers
First edition 1989

ISBN 0 620 13409 7

The Woman's World Cookbook was born because it was a way of celebrating the relationship between the programme and its audience – you, the listeners, were invited to send in your own recipes for a competition that would result in a book to treasure, a book of South African favourite recipes.

Why a cookbook? Because food has always been one of the most popular subjects on the programme, bringing in the greatest audience response. And cookery personalities – affectionately known as "foodies" – have featured frequently in Woman's World interviews over the years. A cookbook seemed the obvious way to extend that participation to our listeners.

We must have been right – because the entries simply streamed in, overwhelmingly from women listeners, though with a few intrepid male cooks thrown in. We had invited recipes for six categories: Soups and Pâtés; Salads; Fish and Seafood; Outdoor Cooking; Meat, Game and Poultry; and Desserts. The enormous task of sorting and selecting from the thousands of recipes was entrusted to eminent "foodie" and broadcasting personality Isabel Jones, who then, with a panel of expert testers, spent weeks testing the recipes chosen.

In the course of testing, suggestions from the experts for improvements and alteration were incorporated wherever necessary to enhance a recipe's usefulness for all cooks out there. Someone who uses a favourite recipe constantly doesn't always realise how they may adjust ingredients here and there, or that an outsider might miss a vital step that's not made clear. So the recipes have been polished and perfected, and this cookbook is the result.

As we hoped, these 170-odd recipes reflect the tastes and eating styles of South Africans today. Some pronounced regional flavours emerged: the Eastern Cape and Transvaal were strong on game; the entire Cape province on fresh fish and seafood; the Transvaal starred again for braais and potjiekos; while Natal was particularly good at delicious salads and desserts with refreshing tropical touches.

But listeners from all over Southern Africa – including Swaziland! – displayed an appreciation of traditional food and skill in developing newer recipes in order to use and enjoy to the full the special bounty of this subcontinent. We hope everyone who uses the book will find it a fascinating exploration of the food South Africans make in their homes, for family and special occasions: well loved recipes that you will want to try for yourselves.

*Marilyn Verster*          *Hilary Reynolds*

Woman's World is a South African radio magazine programme with a wide and faithful audience. Broadcast every weekday morning after the 11 o'clock news on the English service, it is presented by Marilyn Verster and Hilary Reynolds.

# The Winning Touch

A prize for the winning recipe in each category was generously donated by Woolworths, in the form of valuable food vouchers. Woolworths also kindly provided ingredients and wines for judging day, when these winning recipes were selected:

SOUPS & PÂTÉS: Cream of Carrot & Broccoli Soup
(Helena Glennie of Somerset East)

SALADS: Pea & Bacon Salad
(Jean McAllan of Cathcart)

FISH & SEAFOOD: Tropical Fried Fish
(Helena Glennie of Somerset East)

OUTDOOR COOKING: Mushroom Quiche with Waterblommetjies
(Norma Coetzee of Stellenbosch)

MEAT, GAME & POULTRY: Golden Chicken with Honey Mustard Sauce
(Cynthia Koning of Parow)

DESSERTS: Bavarois with Cape Gooseberries
(A Walker of Pietermaritzburg)

Silwood Kitchen, the well known Cape Town cookery school, arranged for a team of top teachers to oversee its best students cooking and expertly presenting the recipes for the judges, who included: Silwood Kitchen's own doyenne, Mrs Lesley Faull; Isabel Jones, cookery expert and media personality, who selected the recipes for this book; Marilyn Verster and Hilary Reynolds, presenters of Woman's World for the SABC; Chris Milne, Development Chef for Woolworths; Peter Veldsman, cookbook author and food editor for *Sarie* magazine; and Lynne Bryer, publisher, Chameleon Press.

Judges' considerations included flavour, texture, appearance, originality and/or interesting use of South African ingredients. The winning recipes and several others in each category were photographed for this book by Roger Bell on behalf of Woolworths, and styled by Isabel Jones. For a list of entrants whose recipes have been published in this book, see the last page.

# Starters

(Soups & Pâtés)

## Starters

*Hot Soups*
Black Bean Soup, 11
Bonnievale Broth, 14
Carrot & Mint Soup, 10
Cauliflower Cheese Soup, 15
Cream of Carrot & Broccoli Soup, 9
Creamy Seafood Bisque, 10
Fresh Watercress Soup, 9
Green Pepper Soup, 13
Haddock & Orange Soup, 12
Pumpkin & Rice Soup, 11
Rich Mushroom & Parsley Soup, 15
Venison Soup, 16
Winter Potato Soup, 13

*Cold Soups*
Cold Apricot Soup, 14
Cold Green Pea Soup, 12

*Pâtés*
Brandied Cream Cheese & Cheddar Roll, 22
Biltong Pâté, 16
Chicken Liver Pâté with a Surprise, 17
Clam & Tuna Pâté, 21
Crab & Salmon Pâté, 20
Herbed Pork & Chicken Liver Terrine, 22
Moulded Chicken Liver Pâté, 21
Mushroom & Blue Cheese Pâté, 17
Smoked Angelfish or Snoek Pâté, 17
Smoked Mackerel Pâté, 16
Smoked Salmon & Avocado Roll, 20

# Cream of Carrot & Broccoli Soup

(Illustrated on page 17)

Serves 4–6

An outstanding recipe for a soup that is really two soups: one green, one orange, served together strikingly as a feast for the eye and the palate.

*400 g carrots*
*400 g broccoli*
*2 onions, chopped*
*50 g butter*
*Freshly ground pepper to taste*
*5 ml (1t) sugar*
*2 medium potatoes, peeled & sliced*
*1 litre chicken stock*
*250 ml (1 cup) cream (more if needed)*
*Chopped chives to garnish*

Peel and chop carrots. Trim broccoli and chop small. Sauté the onions in the butter, using two saucepans and dividing both onion and butter between them. Add the carrots to one saucepan, and the broccoli to the other, stirring over the heat. Season both vegetables to taste (do not add salt if you are using a stock cube); add the sugar to the carrots. Divide the sliced potatoes between the pots, stirring to mix. Now add the warm chicken stock, dividing it between the carrots and the broccoli; simmer for about 30 minutes. Test each pot for seasoning.

Puree each soup separately in the blender until smooth. Finally add half the cream to each and return to their separate pots to heat through. (If the soup is too thick, thin with a little extra cream – but remember that the soups need to remain separate at the serving stage.)

Pour both soups carefully into individual serving bowls, either half and half, or putting in the broccoli soup as a base and the carrot soup in the centre. Garnish with the chopped chives and a swirl of cream.

*Eastern Cape*

# Fresh Watercress Soup

Serves 6

A beautiful, delicate soup served warm with a grating of nutmeg for piquancy.

*1 generous bunch watercress*
*4 leeks, well washed & sliced thinly*
*5 medium potatoes, sliced thinly*
*1 onion, sliced thinly*
*3 cloves garlic, chopped finely*
*15 ml (1T) butter*
*15 ml (1T) olive or sunflower oil*
*1 litre chicken stock*
*750 ml full cream milk*
*250 ml (1 cup) cream*
*Lemon juice to taste*
*Salt & freshly ground black pepper to taste*

MUSHROOM GARNISH
*300 g button mushrooms*
*50 g butter*
*60 ml (1/4 cup) white wine*

Wash, drain and chop the watercress. Melt the butter and oil in a large heavy-based saucepan and sauté the leeks, potatoes, onion and garlic until just golden. Add the stock and simmer gently for 35 minutes, or until the potatoes are tender. Add the watercress, reserving some leaves for the garnish. Stir soup and simmer for another 5–10 minutes. Liquidise in a blender, and strain back into the saucepan. Add the milk, cream, lemon juice and seasoning to taste.

FOR THE GARNISH: Slice the mushrooms thinly and sauté in the butter. When soft, add the wine and simmer until all the liquid has evaporated.

Heat the soup through and garnish with the mushrooms and reserved watercress leaves. A grating of fresh nutmeg can be added. Serve with fresh wholewheat bread and butter.

*Western Cape*

# Carrot & Mint Soup

Serves 6
Mint enhances the flavour of this delicate orange-coloured soup.

*1 kg carrots, sliced*
*4 large onions, chopped*
*2 medium potatoes, sliced*
*2 sticks celery, chopped*
*50 g butter or margarine*
*1 large clove garlic, crushed*
*1-1½ litres hot water*
*5 ml (1t) sugar (optional)*
*Salt & Freshly ground black pepper to taste*
*60 ml (4T) finely chopped fresh parsley*
*60 ml (4T) finely chopped mint leaves*
*250 ml (1 cup) cream, or less to taste*

Add the prepared vegetables to the butter melted in a large saucepan. Add the garlic and stir until the vegetables are coated in butter. Cover pot and cook over low heat for 15 minutes, stirring occasionally to prevent the vegetables from sticking or browning. This "sweating" of the vegetables is important to bring out their full flavour, as the soup does not use stock or stock cubes.

Add the water, sugar, salt and pepper. Cover, bring to the boil and simmer gently for about 15 minutes until the vegetables are tender. Stir in the parsley and mint, and liquidise the soup in a blender. Check for seasoning again, and if soup is too thick add a little hot water. You might like to add some freshly ground black pepper at this stage. Heat soup through and add the cream; do not allow to boil. Serve with a sprig of mint in each bowl.

*Transvaal*

# Creamy Seafood Bisque

Serves 6
A tasty seafood treat that freezes well (omit the cream and shrimps and add when soup is reheated). For the fish, use a firm white fish like kingklip, kabeljou or Cape salmon.

*300 g firm white fish*
*100 g crab meat*
*100 g shrimps*
*45 ml (3T) butter*
*1 medium onion, chopped*
*1 medium carrot, grated*
*1 clove garlic, chopped*
*1 litre water*
*45 ml (3T) sherry*
*150 ml white wine*
*30 ml (2T) tomato paste*
*5 ml (1t) dried mixed herbs*
*250 ml (1 cup) cream*

Cut the fish into bite-sized pieces, removing skin and bones. Flake the crab meat (which may be canned). Cook the shrimps, peel and set aside to add at the very end with the cream. Heat the butter in a large heavy-based saucepan and sauté the onion, carrot and garlic until soft. Add the water, sherry, white wine, tomato paste and mixed herbs. Cover and simmer over low heat for about 45 minutes. Add the cream and only now stir in the peeled shrimps; heat soup through but do not allow to boil. Serve very hot with crusty wholewheat bread and butter.

*Natal*

# Pumpkin & Rice Soup

Serves 6
Pumpkin soup is always delicious – choose a good, sweet Boer pumpkin that isn't watery.

*600 g pumpkin flesh, cubed*
*250 g tomatoes*
*1,5 litres chicken stock*
*30 ml (2T) butter or margarine*
*1 large onion, sliced*
*15 ml (1T) flour*
*80 ml (1/3 cup) uncooked rice*
*1 clove*
*Freshly ground black pepper*
*2 ml (1/2t) turmeric*
*2 ml (1/2t) ground or grated nutmeg*

GARNISH
*15 ml (1T) lemon juice*
*45 ml (3T) cream*

Cube the pumpkin flesh and skin and chop the tomatoes; keep aside. Have the chicken stock ready to add to the soup while warm. Melt the butter in a large saucepan and sauté the onion for a few minutes. Sprinkle on the flour, stir and cook another minute. Remove pot from heat and add the warm stock gradually, stirring. Add the pumpkin, tomatoes, rice and seasonings. Return to the heat and bring to the boil, then cover and simmer gently for about 30 minutes, stirring every now and then.

Liquidise soup in a blender, or rub through a sieve. Reheat the soup, test for seasoning (you may need to add salt) and pour into the serving bowl or bowls. Mix the lemon juice and cream and swirl across the top of the soup.

*Transvaal*

# Black Bean Soup

Serves 8–10
Another substantial winter treat, using a smoked pork hock and adding Madeira wine near the end. Ideal for making ahead, as it improves by being kept overnight – and freezes well.

*500 g black or sugar beans*
*30 g butter*
*1 carrot, chopped*
*2 sticks celery, chopped finely*
*2 onions, chopped*
*3 leeks, chopped*
*1 smoked pork hock (or use chopped bacon)*
*3 litres brown meat stock*
*1 bayleaf*
*Salt & black pepper to taste*
*250 ml (1 cup) sweet Madeira wine*
*100 ml finely chopped parsley*
*2 hard-boiled eggs, sliced as garnish*
*Lemon slices to garnish*

Cover beans with cold water in a large saucepan; bring to the boil and cook for 5 minutes. Remove from heat and leave to stand for 1 hour. Drain off all liquid.

Melt the butter in another large saucepan and sauté the carrot, celery, onion and leeks for a few minutes. Add the smoked hock, the beans, stock, bayleaf and salt and pepper. Simmer over low heat until both beans and pork are tender (2–3 hours).

Remove the bayleaf and the bone and rind from the hock. Liquidise the soup to the desired consistency, in a blender or processor. Return to the pot, heat through and add the chopped parsley and the Madeira wine.

Black bean soup is traditionally served garnished with slices of hardboiled eggs and lemon. Wholewheat bread completes a satisfying winter meal.

*Natal*

## Haddock & Orange Soup

Serves 6
A rich, slightly sweet soup made from the unusual combination of carrot, fresh oranges and smoked haddock.

*300 g smoked haddock fillets*
*500 g carrots*
*1 large onion*
*30 ml (2T) butter*
*500 ml (2 cups) chicken stock*
*125 ml (1/2 cup) fresh orange juice*
*5 ml (1t) orange rind, grated*
*Freshly ground black pepper to taste*
*60 ml (1/4 cup) dry sherry*
*125 ml (1/2 cup) cream*
*Salt as needed*
*Fresh parsley for garnish*

Poach haddock in cold water for 10 minutes; drain, discarding skin and bones. Flake and set aside. Peel and chop the carrots, and chop the onion. Melt the butter in a large saucepan and add the carrots and onion; sauté them until soft but not browned. Stir in the stock, orange juice and rind and some freshly ground black pepper. Simmer gently until the carrots are really soft.

Liquidise the soup in a blender. Reheat in the saucepan, and then add the sherry, the cream and the flaked haddock. Heat through and test for seasoning – you may need to add salt. If the soup is too thick, thin with a little milk. Serve hot, garnished with a little fresh parsley chopped finely.

*Natal*

## Cold Green Pea Soup

Serves 6
An attractive soup using lettuce as well as frozen peas.

*400 g frozen green peas*
*1 lettuce*
*1 medium potato*
*1 medium onion*
*600 ml chicken stock*
*45 ml (3T) sherry*
*Juice of half a lemon*
*Salt & black pepper to taste*
*125 ml (1/2 cup) cream*
*Sprigs of fresh mint for garnish*

Frozen peas are easy, but there is no reason why you shouldn't use fresh green peas if available. Wash and quarter the lettuce, and peel and slice the potato and onion. Place half the chicken stock in a large saucepan and bring to the boil with the vegetables. Cover and simmer until the potatoes are cooked.

Liquidise the soup in a blender and return to the pot. Add the remaining stock and the sherry, heat through and simmer for 5 minutes. Stir in the lemon juice and test for seasoning. Finally stir in most of the cream and then chill the soup well before serving. Garnish each helping with a swirl of the remaining cream and a sprig of mint.

*Natal*

# Winter Potato Soup

Serves 6
A very flavoursome soup – for vegetarians, substitute vegetable stock and add 2 ml (1/2t) powdered cumin in place of the bacon.

*1 kg potatoes*
*4 onions, chopped*
*30 ml (2T) butter*
*1,5 litres water*
*3 chicken stock cubes*
*100 g bacon, chopped*
*150 ml cream*
*250 ml (1 cup) sour cream/Smetena (optional)*
*Freshly ground white pepper*
*Chopped chives for garnish*

Peel and cube the potatoes. Melt the butter in a large saucepan and "sweat" the onions in it until soft and transparent (this will take about 15–20 minutes and should be done over the gentlest heat). When the onions are really soft and melting, add the cubed potatoes. Cook, stirring, for a few minutes. Then add the water and stock cubes. Cover, bring to the boil, then lower heat and leave to simmer for 25 minutes.

Liquidise the soup in a blender or processor until smooth. Add the bacon and simmer for a further 15 minutes. Add the fresh cream and reheat soup until just below boiling point. Remove from heat, whisk in the sour cream and serve immediately, sprinkling each bowl with the chopped chives.

*Western Cape*

# Green Pepper Soup
(Illustrated on page 17)

Serves 6
A striking soup using a vegetable that is widely available and often economical. For the best colour – and the most delicate flavour – use a homemade chicken stock.

*1 litre chicken stock*
*4 large green peppers, seeded & chopped*
*2 large onions, chopped*
*15 ml (1T) butter or margarine*
*15 ml (1T) cooking oil*
*15 ml (1T) flour*
*Salt & freshly ground pepper to taste*
*250 ml (1 cup) milk, cream or sour cream/Smetena*
*Chopped chives to garnish*

Have ready the chicken stock. Sauté the green pepper and onion in the butter and oil, using a large heavy-based pot. Sprinkle over the flour and stir until smooth, cooking for 1 minute. Add the chicken stock gradually, bring to the boil, then reduce heat and simmer for 5 minutes. Transfer to the blender and process until smooth.

Return the soup to the pot, season to taste and stir in the milk or cream. Cook over low heat, stirring constantly, until soup is heated through – do not allow to boil. Pour into serving bowls and garnish with chopped chives.

*Transvaal*

# Cold Apricot Soup

Serves 6
Cold fruit soups are more common in Europe than in Africa, despite the climate – an acquired taste!

*500 ml (2 cups) dried apricots*
*750 ml water*
*15 ml (1T) honey*
*5 ml (1t) lemon juice*
*2 ml (1/2t) salt, or to taste*
*2 ml (1/2t) ground cinnamon*
*2 ml (1/2t) grated nutmeg*
*375 ml milk*
*250 ml (1 cup) cream*
*Grated lemon rind*

Soak the apricots overnight in the water. Bring to the boil in the same water and simmer for about 30 minutes. Liquidise in a blender.

Add the honey, lemon juice, salt and spices. Cool. Just before serving, stir in the chilled milk and cream, and top with the grated lemon rind.

(If you wish to serve this soup warm, heat gently after liquidising, add the flavourings and lastly the milk and cream; heat through without boiling.)

*Eastern Cape*

# Bonnievale Broth

Serves 8
A hearty winter treat, this is pea soup with a difference. If you don't have a pressure cooker, use the slow method and your soup will taste just as good.

*250 ml (1 cup) dried split peas*
*2 litres cold water*
*1 beef stock cube*
*250 g smoked sausage (eg Russians)*
*1 large carrot, grated*
*1 large potato, grated*
*1 large clove garlic, crushed*
*2 bayleaves*
*Salt & freshly ground black pepper to taste*
*15 ml (1T) flour mixed with 250 ml (1 cup) milk*
*100 ml dry white wine*
*50 g finely grated cheddar cheese for garnish*

Wash the dried peas and soak overnight in water; drain. Place peas in pressure cooker with the 2 litres cold water and the beef stock cube (crumbled). Close securely and pressure-cook for 20 minutes. Reduce pressure by cooling cooker in cold water. (Cooks using the stove must simmer the peas till soft – about 1 hour or more.)

Slice the sausage in 1cm slices and add to the soup with the grated carrot and potato, the garlic and the bayleaves. Stir. Pressure-cook for 10 minutes, reducing pressure as before. (On the stove, simmer for another 30 minutes.) Season to taste with salt and pepper.

While the soup simmers uncovered, thicken (if necessary) with the flour and milk. Finally add the wine, heat through and serve in bowls, garnished with the grated cheese.

Homebaked wholewheat bread completes a winter treat that is a meal in itself.

*Overberg, Cape*

# Cauliflower Cheese Soup

Serves 4
A smooth, velvety soup – you could add a little grated nutmeg for more spiciness.

*500 g cauliflower*
*1 small onion, chopped*
*30 ml (2T) butter*
*500 ml (2 cups) chicken stock*
*250 ml (1 cup) milk*
*Freshly ground white pepper*
*80 ml (1/3 cup) cream*
*250 ml (1 cup) grated cheddar cheese*
*Chopped chives to garnish*

Trim and chop the cauliflower. Melt the butter in a large saucepan and sauté the onion until soft and golden. Add the cauliflower and stir well over the heat. Add the chicken stock and milk and bring almost to the boil, then simmer carefully for for 20 minutes – watch the pot, as it tends to boil over. Liquidise. Return to the pot, add the cream and heat through (do not boil). If the soup is too thick, you may thin it with additional milk. Test for seasoning – if you used homemade stock you may need to add salt. Now add the grated cheese and turn off the heat, stirring to melt the cheese. When soup is smooth, serve sprinkled with the chives.

*Western Cape*

# Rich Mushroom & Parsley Soup
(Illustrated on page 17)

Serves 6
A rich and fairly extravagant soup – but quite worth the expense! The flavour is superb.

*750 g black mushrooms*
*100 g fresh parsley*
*100 g butter*
*2 cloves garlic, crushed*
*5 slices white bread (no crusts)*
*1 litre good chicken stock*
*Salt & pepper to taste*
*Grated nutmeg or ground mace*
*125–250 ml (1/2–1 cup) cream*

Wipe mushrooms and chop roughly. Chop the parsley finely.

Melt the butter in a large saucepan and add the mushrooms, parsley and garlic; stir. Cover and cook slowly for 10 minutes. Crumble the bread into the saucepan. Add the stock and seasonings (if you use a stock cube, be careful not to add too much salt.) Heat up, stirring, and simmer for 10 minutes. Liquidise the soup in a blender, pour into a clean saucepan and add the cream. Reheat gently (do not boil). Serve hot with crusty bread.

*Eastern Cape*

# Venison Soup

Serves 6

Venison soup, packed with vegetables, is an unusual treat, and great for using up bones or even cheaper stewing cuts. Use fresh vegetables instead of the frozen ones when a good selection – peas, green beans, broccoli, cauliflower – is available.

*500 g venison shank bones*
*500 ml brown sugar beans*
*2 large onions, chopped*
*5 carrots, sliced*
*500 ml (2 cups) frozen vegetables (see above)*
*1 large tomato, peeled & chopped*
*1 beef stock cube*
*5 ml (1t) dried origanum or marjoram*
*2 ml (1/2 t) dried rosemary or sage*
*5 ml (1t) whole black peppercorns*
*2 ml (1/2t) ground allspice*
*15 ml (1T) quince jelly*
*Salt and pepper to taste*

Place the bones, beans, vegetables (chopped if fresh), plus all the spices and seasonings in a large soup pot and cover well with cold water. Add salt and pepper to taste. Cover the pot and bring to the boil, then reduce heat and simmer for a good few hours – this is a soup designed for the anthracite or woodburning stoves on farms! The soup sould be thick, and freezes well (remove the bones), improving in flavour with reheating.

*Eastern Cape*

*Opposite: (from bottom clockwise)* Cream of Carrot & Broccoli Soup, Rich Mushroom & Parsley Soup, and *(top)* Green Pepper Soup
*Overleaf: (from bottom clockwise)* Brandied Cream Cheese & Cheddar Roll, Moulded Chicken Liver Pâté, and Biltong Pâté
*Prepared with choice ingredients from Woolworths food markets*

# Smoked Mackerel Pâté

Serves 4–6

Smoked mackerel is available at supermarkets. If you use the peppered fillets, you will not need to add any pepper to this rich pâté. Smoked angelfish could be used as a substitute, increasing the amount of cream.

*200 g smoked mackerel fillets*
*50 g butter, softened*
*15 ml (1T) creamed horseradish*
*45 ml (3T) cream*
*Freshly ground black pepper*

Skin, debone and mash the mackerel fillets. Mix with the softened butter, horseradish and cream, adding plenty of freshly ground black pepper to taste. Pile into a suitable bowl.

If the pâté is to be kept for a day or two, or frozen, seal the top with melted butter flavoured with lemon juice and finely chopped parsley.

Serve with freshly baked wholewheat bread, melba toast or unsalted biscuits.

*Natal*

# Biltong Pâté
(Illustrated on page 18)

Serves 4-6

A very South African pâté. Other kinds of game biltong could also be used – just be careful that you do not use an over salty biltong, which will dominate the pâté. A light dash of gin makes a zesty addition.

*100 g kudu biltong, grated finely*
*100 g smooth cream cheese*
*50 ml cream, or more to taste*
*10 ml (2t) Worcestershire sauce*
*1 ml (1/4t) ground coriander*

Mix all the ingredients well together – the saltier the biltong, the more cream will be needed. As this is a fairly loose pâté, it can be piped into attractive shapes, or simply spooned into ramekins or little bowls. Serve with melba toast or freshly baked brown bread.

*Eastern Cape*

## Chicken Liver Pâté with a Surprise

Serves 6
Bacon, tomato puree and plenty of flavouring make this chicken liver pâté different – make it as a baked terrine or as the usual softer version.

*250 g chicken livers*
*125 g rindless bacon*
*2 large onions*
*45 ml (3T) butter*
*3 large cloves garlic, crushed*
*10 ml (2t) fresh marjoram, chopped*
*4 drops Tabasco*
*5 ml (1t) salt*
*Freshly ground black pepper to taste*
*75 ml tomato puree*
*30 ml (2T) sweet sherry*
*15 ml (1T) fresh parsley, chopped finely*
*15 ml (1T) fresh chives, chopped finely*
*1 egg & a little butter (for the baked terrine)*

Trim the chicken livers, discarding any greenish pieces. Chop the rindless bacon finely. Chop the onions. In a large frying pan, melt the butter and sauté the onions gently until transparent. Add the bacon and sauté until it is cooked but not crisp. Add the garlic and the prepared chicken livers, and fry until the livers are cooked on the outside but still pink in the middle. Add the marjoram, Tabasco, salt and black pepper to taste, tomato puree and sherry; stir well over the heat. Add the parsley and chives and stir again, cooking for a minute longer.

FOR A TERRINE: At this stage, blend the mixture well with the egg in a blender or food processor. Pour into an ovenproof terrine or dish with a lid, smooth the surface and dot with a little butter to keep the surface from drying out. Cover, place the dish in a pan of warm water to come about halfway up the sides, and bake in oven preheated to 160 °C for about 40 minutes or until set. Cool and refrigerate before serving.

FOR A SOFTER VERSION: Blend the cooked mixture in a blender or food processor, pour into a suitable serving bowl and cover with plastic wrap; refrigerate until needed (pâtés improve with keeping – overnight is best, but this pâté may be kept in the fridge for up to a week if covered).

Serve both pâtés with crusty bread, melba toast or biscuits.

*Orange Free State*

## Smoked Angelfish or Snoek Pâté

Serves 6
A Cape favourite, best made with unfrozen smoked fish which has better flavour and consistency.

*250 g smoked angelfish or snoek*
*30 ml (2T) mayonnaise*
*45 ml (3T) cream, or to taste*
*5 ml (1t) lemon juice*
*Freshly ground black pepper*

Debone and flake the smoked fish finely, discarding any thick or dark skin. Using a fork, blend with the mayonnaise (which should be good quality – use less if your mayonnaise has a sharp taste) and enough cream to make a pleasantly loose pâté. (You may blend the ingredients in a blender if you prefer a smoother pâté.) Season with the lemon juice and sufficient black pepper for a tangy result. Place in a bowl, cover and chill. Serve with melba toast or unsalted biscuits. This is also good with wholewheat bread for a light lunch.

*Western Cape*

# Smoked Salmon & Avocado Roll

Serves 8

An elegant starter – for professional slices, dip a sharp knife in boiling water before cutting.

*250 g smoked salmon*
*1 medium avocado*
*250 g cream cheese*
*45 ml (3T) prepared horseradish*
*30 ml (2T) lemon juice*
*1 envelope (10 g) plain gelatine*
*Salt & freshly ground black pepper to taste*
*Grated lemon rind for garnish*
*Fresh parsley, chopped, for garnish*

Choose smoked salmon that is thinly sliced. The avocado should be ripe. Blend the flesh of the avocado with the cream cheese and the horseradish until smooth. Put the lemon juice in a small saucepan and sprinkle the gelatine over it; when it has caked or "sponged", heat gently over low heat until the gelatine dissolves. Add to the avocado/cream cheese mixture and mix well together. Pour into a bowl set over a larger bowl containing ice, and stir with a wooden spoon until the mixture is thick. Add salt and freshly ground black pepper to taste.

Place a sheet of plastic cling wrap 20 cm long on the table or counter, and lay the smoked salmon slices on it, overlapping slightly and leaving a narrow border either side. Spread the avocado mixture on the salmon and carefully roll up as if for a Swiss roll, tucking the edges of the plastic wrap in so that the whole is covered. Chill for several hours until firm. Remove wrap and with a sharp knife (see above) cut the roll into 1 cm slices. Place 2 or 3 slices on each individual plate (you could line them with lettuce leaves) and garnish with the grated lemon rind and chopped parsley.

*Eastern Cape*

# Crab & Salmon Pâté

Serves 6

Crab is not always easy to obtain, but combines with canned salmon for a very pleasant starter.

*1 × 200 g can pink salmon*
*1 × 180 g or 200 g can crab*
*60 g butter*
*30 ml (2T) flour*
*125 ml (1/2 cup) milk*
*125 ml (1/2 cup) cream*
*80 ml (1/3 cup) sherry or white wine*
*5 ml (1t) French mustard*
*Salt and freshly ground pepper to taste*
*Dash of Tabasco*
*15 ml (1T) gelatine*
*60 ml (1/4 cup) water*

Skin and debone the salmon, reserving the juices. Drain and flake the crab meat; set aside.

Melt the butter in a frying pan, add the flour and stir well to mix. Remove from the heat, add the milk and cream and stir until combined (a balloon whisk is useful here). Return pan to heat and stir until the sauce thickens. Simmer about 2 minutes longer, then remove from heat, stir in the sherry or wine and the mustard, and season well with salt and pepper to taste. A drop or two of Tabasco would add extra flavour here.

Add the gelatine to the cold water and leave until it has caked or "sponged"; add to the white sauce and return sauce to the heat, stirring for a few minutes – but do NOT allow the sauce to boil. Pour the sauce into a blender or processor and add the salmon and its juices; blend until smooth. Remove the mixture from the blender and add the flaked crab meat, mixing in carefully with a wooden spoon. Pour mixture into individual ramekins or bowls, cover and refrigerate for several hours or overnight.

*Transvaal*

# Mushroom & Blue Cheese Pâté

Serves 6–8
A rich pâté useful for vegetarian occasions.

*125 g black mushrooms*
*125 g blue cheese (Blaauwkrantz)*
*125 g smooth cottage cheese*
*15 ml (1T) fresh chives, chopped finely*
*10 ml (2t) fresh parsley, chopped finely*
*Few drops Tabasco*
*Salt & freshly ground black pepper to taste*

Grate the mushrooms or chop very finely (a food processor is a help). Grate the blue cheese with a fine grater. Mix both mushrooms and cheese well with the other ingredients. (If the mixture is too thick, thin with a little cream.) Put in a serving bowl and decorate with thinly sliced quarters of mushrooms round the edge. Serve at once, with melba toast or savoury biscuits.

*Transvaal*

# Clam & Tuna Pâté

Serves 6-8
A tasty pâté that will be a hit with guests – yet it is easily and quickly made from the store cupboard.

*1 × 200 g can light meat tuna (in oil)*
*1 × 105 g can smoked clams (in oil)*
*125 ml (1/2 cup) cream*
*125 ml (1/2 cup) grated cheddar cheese*
*60 ml (1/4 cup) dry white wine*
*6 slices white bread, crumbed (no crusts)*
*10 capers*
*45 ml (3T) tomato sauce*
*Half a small onion, chopped*
*1 stick celery, finely chopped*
*2 cloves garlic, crushed*
*2 ml (1/2t) fish masala or curry powder*
*2 ml (1/2t) salt*
*2 ml (1/2t) fine black pepper*

Drain excess oil from the tuna and clams. Combine tuna and clams with the remaining ingredients and process or blend until smooth. Pour into a bowl and cover with plastic wrap; chill before serving. Garnish with sprigs of celery leaves and serve with melba toast.

*Western Cape*

# Moulded Chicken Liver Pâté
(Illustrated on page 18)

Serves 6
An attractive way to serve chicken liver pâté – when chilled, it can be moulded into a shape and, for full effect, covered with slices of pimento-stuffed olives, or simply topped with dried pear slices or dried figs soaked in a little sherry.

*500 g chicken livers*
*90 ml (6T) butter*
*1 small onion, finely chopped*
*30 ml (2T) brandy or sherry*
*2 cloves garlic, crushed*
*5 ml (1t) fresh origanum, chopped*
*(OR 2 ml (1/2t) dried origanum)*
*Little freshly ground nutmeg*
*Salt & freshly ground black pepper to taste*

Trim the livers, discarding any greenish sacs. Melt 30 ml (2T) of the butter in a frying pan and gently cook the livers for about 5 minutes – they should still be pink inside. With a slotted spoon, remove the livers to the blender and process until smooth. To the butter left in the pan, add the onion and the brandy or sherry, and simmer gently. Add the garlic, herbs, nutmeg and salt and pepper to taste, stir up once or twice, then pour all into the blender and process with the livers, adding also the remaining 60 ml (4T) butter. When the pâté is smooth, chill it in a covered container, preferably over-night (the flavour improves with keeping). The pâté will be firm enough to mould to a shape and decorate as desired (see above).

*Western Cape*

## Herbed Pork & Chicken Liver Terrine

Serves 8–10
An outstanding recipe for a moulded terrine that needs to be made at least a day ahead, but will keep for several more.

*250 g chicken livers*
*500 g pork shoulder, minced*
*500 g frozen chopped spinach*
*125 g bacon, finely chopped*
*4 eggs, lightly beaten*
*80 ml (1/3 cup) fresh parsley, chopped*
*2 garlic cloves, crushed*
*20 ml (4t) dried basil*
*15 ml (1T) dried thyme*
*5 ml (1t) salt*
*Nutmeg & pepper to taste*
*15 ml (1T) gelatine*
*80 ml (1/3 cup) sherry*
*250 ml (1 cup) spring onions, chopped*
*45 ml (3T) butter*
*80 ml (1/3 cup) heavy cream*
*60 ml (1/4) cup brandy*
*375 g bacon to line terrine*
*Fresh herbs to garnish*

Trim the chicken livers, removing any green pieces and membranes; cut into pieces (about 1 cm) and set aside. In a large bowl combine the minced pork with the spinach, which should be cooked according to instruction on the box, and squeezed well to drain off excess moisture. Add the chopped bacon, eggs, parsley, garlic, herbs and other seasonings. In a small bowl, sprinkle the gelatine over the sherry and leave to cake or "sponge" for 10 minutes.

Meanwhile in a frying pan cook the spring onions in the butter over moderate heat for 2 minutes. Add the chicken liver pieces and sauté over moderately high heat until they are lightly browned on the outside but still pink inside. Add to the pork mixture, then stir in the gelatine and sherry, and the cream. Deglaze the pan with the brandy, scraping up all the brown bits; add to the pork/liver mixture, combining the ingredients well.

Line a 3 litre terrine with the bacon slices, letting the ends hang over the sides. Fill the terrine with the pork mixture, mounding it slightly in the middle. Fold the overhanging bacon over the top. Cover the terrine with foil and a lid, or a triple layer of foil. Place in a baking pan, add hot water to come halfway up the sides of the terrine and bake in a moderate oven (180 °C) for 2 hours. Remove the terrine from the oven, pour off the water and leave the terrine to stand in the pan for 15 minutes. Then remove the lid, leaving the foil, and weight the terrine with a 2 kg weight (cans of food will do this). Leave to cool, then chill the terrine overnight.

TO UNMOULD: Remove the foil and run a thin knife round the inside of the terrine. Invert a platter over the terrine, and unmould the pâté onto this. Serve sliced, with sprigs of fresh herbs as garnish.

*Transvaal*

## Brandied Cream Cheese & Cheddar Roll
(Illustrated on page 18)

Serves 10–12
A delicious cheesy starter guests will love. Dieters can use smooth cottage cheese instead of the cream cheese – the result is still excellent.

*250 g smooth cream cheese*
*500 ml (2 cups) cheddar cheese, finely grated*
*5 ml (1t) finely grated onion*
*2 ml (1/2t) Worcestershire sauce*
*Few drops Tabasco*
*15 ml (1T) brandy*
*2 ml (1/2t) French mustard*
*Salt & black pepper to taste*
*Chopped pecans or walnuts (about 100 g)*

Use a wooden spoon to blend all the ingredients except the nuts until creamy smooth. Roll into a sausage shape, wrap in greaseproof paper and chill overnight. (The mixture will firm up in the fridge.) When ready to serve, roll in the nuts until coated. Serve with melba toast or unsalted biscuits and a cold white wine.

*Natal*

# Salads

# Salads

Brown Rice & Lentils, 29
Brown Rice Salad, 27
Butternut Salad, 34
Carrot & Banana Salad, 30
Curried Chicken & Fruit Salad, 32
Doc's Salad, 28
Four Bean Salad, 29
Grape & Cheese Salad, 32
Grapefruit & Avocado Salad, 27
Heat Beater Salad, 26
Joan's Layered Salad, 25
Old-Fashioned Potato Salad, 33
Pea & Bacon Salad, 25
Pickled Mushrooms, 20
Potato Skin Salad, 34
Pretty Pear Salad, 31
Seasonal Salad with Blaauwkrantz Balls, 26
Sesame Noodle Salad, 28
Summer Rice Salad, 33
Sweet & Sour Cucumbers, 30
Tuna & Smoked Mussel Salad, 31
Wheat Rice Salad, 27

# Pea & Bacon Salad

(Illustrated on page 35)

Serves 6
Unusual flavours combine in a winning salad with plenty to surprise the palate.

*250 g frozen peas*
*8 slices streaky bacon*
*375 ml (1½ cups) salted peanuts*
*4 stalks celery, chopped*
*1 onion, chopped finely*
*125 ml (1/2 cup) mayonnaise*
*125 ml (1/2 cup) plain yoghurt*
*30 ml (2T) lemon juice*
*Salt to taste*
*Paprika or cayenne pepper to taste*
*1 medium lettuce for salad bed*

Set peas aside to thaw in a bowl. Fry the bacon in a non-stick (or very lightly oiled) frying pan until browned and crisp. Drain on paper towel and cool; then crumble coarsely and set aside.

Mix peas, peanuts, celery, onion, mayonnaise, yoghurt and lemon juice. Sprinkle with salt and paprika or cayenne, and mix lightly. Wash and thoroughly dry the lettuce leaves and arrange in bowl or platter. Pile the salad on the lettuce leaves and scatter the crumbled bacon over. Serve immediately.

*Eastern Cape*

# Joan's Layered Salad

Serves 6–8
A salad that looks lovely through a straight-sided glass bowl, revealing layers of different colours and textures. In winter, you could create a similar effect with cauliflower, broccoli, red and green apples and avocado pear. For a salad luncheon, add a layer of flaked tuna or chopped cold chicken (and add mayonnaise to the dressing).

*3 clingstone peaches, chopped*
*Half an English cucumber, sliced thinly*
*8–10 mushrooms, sliced*
*2 stalks celery, chopped*
*4 medium carrots, cut into matchsticks*
*6–8 courgettes, sliced*
*250 ml (1 cup) cherry tomatoes*
*1 medium green pepper, chopped*
*Bite-size pieces of lettuce*

DRESSING
*125 ml (1/2 cup) salad oil*
*60–125 ml (1/4–1/2 cup) good wine or cider vinegar*
*5 ml (1t) paprika*
*2 ml (1/2t) each onion & garlic salt, or to taste*
*2 ml (1/2t) lemon or black pepper*
*5 ml (1t) dried mixed herbs*
*2 ml (1/2t) mustard powder*
*2 ml (1/2t) brown sugar*

*Toasted sunflower seeds for garnish (optional)*

The chopped peaches should be coated in the dressing before forming the bottom layer of this salad; then add the rest of the salad ingredients, layer by layer, finishing with the lettuce and perhaps an extra sprig of cherry tomatoes.

DRESSING: Mix all ingredients together in a bottle and shake well to blend. Pour over the salad just before serving. Sprinkle the salad with toasted sunflower seeds to add extra crunch and protein.

TOASTED SUNFLOWER SEEDS: Stir into melted butter in a pan; add onion or garlic salt to taste. Fry until golden. Pour into dish lined with paper towel to drain the seeds. When cool, store in an airtight container.

*Western Cape*

## Seasonal Salad with Blaauwkrantz Balls

(Illustrated on page 36)

Serves 6–8
An eye-catching salad that would also make an excellent vegetarian meal – the blue cheese balls are a treat.

*1 butter lettuce*
*250 ml (1 cup) grated cabbage*
*5 large carrots, cut into matchsticks*
*5 sticks celery, cut into slivers*
*1 large Granny Smith apple, diced*
*15 ml (1T) sultanas*
*15 ml (1T) slivered almonds*
*15 ml (1T) fresh parsley, chopped*
*15 ml (1T) salad oil*
*15 ml (1T) cider vinegar*
*Salt & black pepper to taste*

BLUE CHEESE BALLS
*250 g Blaauwkrantz (blue) cheese, grated*
*250 g smooth cream cheese*
*1 medium onion, finely chopped*
*5 ml (1t) chopped chives*
*Ground almonds or crushed pecan nuts to coat*

Wash and dry the lettuce; and shred. Mix with the cabbage, carrot, celery, apple, sultanas and almonds. Mix together the parsley, oil, vinegar and salt and pepper to taste; pour over the salad and toss. Arrange salad in salad bowl or on platter.

CHEESE BALLS: Mix all the ingredients except the nuts. Form the mixture into small balls (about 2 cm in diameter) and roll the balls in the nuts. (If you use ground almonds, you will need a little paprika to add colour to the balls.) Arrange on and around the salad.

NOTE: You could slice the cheese balls onto the salad for daintier helpings.

*Natal*

## Heat Beater Salad

Serves 4–6
A green salad with a refreshing yoghurt dressing, good to look at and a pleasant side dish for curry.

*1 small lettuce, shredded*
*1 cucumber, peeled, seeded & grated*
*1 large tomato, peeled & chopped*
*1 × 175 ml tub plain (Bulgarian) yoghurt*
*30 ml (2T) fresh mint, finely chopped*
*30 ml (2T) parsley, finely chopped*
*15 ml (1T) chopped chives*
*Salt & black pepper to taste*

Line a salad bowl with the lettuce. Sprinkle the grated cucumber with a little salt and press with a weight to draw out as much liquid as possible; drain well and arrange the cucumber on the lettuce. Add the chopped tomato (which you might like to sprinkle with a very little sugar first), and any juice. Stir the herbs into the yoghurt, add salt and pepper and pour over the salad. Toss gently and serve.

*Western Cape*

# Brown Rice Salad

Serves 6–8
Fruity brown rice makes a healthy salad to accompany the traditional South African braai.

*750 ml (3 cups) cooked brown rice*
*750 ml (3 cups) chopped fresh pineapple*
*250 ml (1 cup) chopped celery*
*125 ml (1/2 cup) chopped green pepper*
*1 onion finely chopped*
*45 ml (3T) finely chopped parsley*
*60 ml (4T) seedless raisins or sultanas*
*125 ml (1/2 cup) sunflower seeds*

DRESSING
*125 ml (1/2 cup) salad oil*
*30 ml (2T) lemon juice*
*5 ml (1t) curry powder*
*5 ml (1t) soy sauce*
*15 ml (1T) honey*

Mix salad ingredients in a large bowl. Combine dressing ingredients and shake well to blend; pour over the salad and toss to mix. Chill in the refrigerator until needed.

*Natal*

# Grapefruit & Avocado Salad

Serves 4
A good salad to serve with fish, or as a starter.

*3 grapefruit*
*1 large ripe avocado (or 2 small)*
*1 Granny Smith apple*
*1 bunch green grapes, peeled & seeded (optional)*
*50 ml French dressing*
*4 sprigs mint*

Cut top and bottom off grapefruit with a sharp knife. Cut away all peel and pith with downward strokes. Cut between membranes to release each segment, then place this flesh in a bowl with any juice. Halve the avocado and cube. Add to the bowl and coat with the juice. Dice the apple and add, again turning to coat with juice. If they are in season, add the peeled and seeded grapes. Chill.

TO SERVE: Add the French dressing and decorate with sprigs of fresh mint. Or divide into four individual bowls, adding grapefruit juice and a spoon of French dressing to each, and a sprig of mint. (NOTE: Cooked, diced potato may be substituted for any of the ingredients except the grapefruit.)

*Natal*

# Wheat Rice Salad

Serves 6
Wheat rice makes a satisfying base for a fruit-flavoured salad with a curry tang. If wheat rice is unavailable, use brown or even white rice.

*500 g wheat rice kernels*
*1 × 410 g can peach slices*
*60 ml (4T) sultanas*
*6 pickled onions, chopped*
*6 gherkins, chopped*
*30 ml (2T) chutney*
*10 ml (2t) curry powder*
*30 ml (2T) smooth apricot jam*
*250 ml (1 cup) mayonnaise*

Cook the wheat rice in lightly salted water until tender. Drain and allow to cool in a large bowl. Drain the peach slices, reserving the juice; chop the peaches and add to the wheat rice with the sultanas (these can be soaked beforehand in water, if desired), pickled onions and gherkins. Mix the reserved peach juice with the chutney, curry powder, jam and mayonnaise. Pour over the salad and toss. Chill until needed.

*Transvaal*

## Doc's Salad

Serves 4–6
An attractive salad with a good combination of ingredients.

*1 Granny Smith apple, diced*
*3 slices pineapple, diced*
*3 slices (about 40 g) mature cheddar cheese, diced*
*Quarter of an English cucumber, diced*
*Half an avocado (when available), diced*
*1 cup lettuce, shredded finely*
*Toasted almonds*
*45 ml (1T) sultanas*

In a large glass bowl, layer the salad ingredients: Start with the apple, then pineapple, cheese, cucumber, avocado, and finally the lettuce, to cover the other ingredients. (Butter lettuce is also good with this salad.) Sprinkle with the toasted nuts and the sultanas. Do not toss or stir or add any dressing or lemon juice. This will keep the salad from turning soggy, and when you serve it the salad will automatically be mixed. (You may serve a dressing separately.) Cover the salad and chill; this salad goes well with tuna and mayonnaise or salad cream.

*Western Cape*

## Sesame Noodle Salad
(Illustrated on page 46)

Serves 6
A most attractive medley of vegetables and noodles, with the nutty surprise of toasted sesame seeds. An excellent choice for vegetarians.

*250 g medium shell noodles*
*2 carrots, peeled & cut into matchsticks*
*2 large spring onions, sliced (green part too)*
*1 medium green pepper, diced*

DRESSING
*80 ml (1/3 cup) sunflower oil*
*80 ml (1/3 cup) cider vinegar*
*45 ml (3T) soy sauce*
*30 ml (2T) roasted peanut powder\**
*5 ml (1t) brown sugar*
*2 ml (1/2t) salt*
*2 ml (1/2t) mustard powder*
*2 ml (1/2t) sesame oil*
*2 ml (1/2t) green root ginger, chopped finely*
*Freshly ground black pepper*

GARNISH
*60 ml (1/4 cup) toasted sesame seeds*
*250 ml (1 cup) fresh spinach, shredded*

*\* To make your own roasted peanut powder, buy roasted peanuts and grind to a powder in the processor.*

Cook the noodles in plenty of salted, fast boiling water until still firm to the bite (al dente). Drain, and rinse in cold water; drain again well.

Combine all the ingredients for the dressing in a jar and shake well to mix. Toss together the noodles, carrots, spring onions and green pepper. Pour the dressing over and mix. Cover and refrigerate salad overnight, if possible, to marinate. Toss from time to time.

Just before serving, toast sesame seeds in a dry pan. (Don't let them burn!) Add to the salad together with the shredded spinach.

*Natal*

# Four Bean Salad

Serves 10–12
A quick and easy salad from canned beans, this should be made a day ahead for flavours to mature. Excellent for serving at a large braai.

*Any 4 of these 410 g cans of beans:*
*Red kidney beans (good for colour)*
*Pinto beans*
*Lima beans*
*Baked beans in tomato sauce*
*Green beans*
*Butter beans*

*125 ml (1/2 cup) salad oil*
*125 ml (1/2 cup) cider vinegar*
*180 ml (2/3 cup) sugar*
*5 ml (1t) salt*
*125 ml (1/2 cup) chopped onion*
*125 ml (1/2 cup) chopped green pepper*

Drain the beans in a colander. Heat the oil, vinegar and sugar in a saucepan; add the salt. Do not allow to boil. In a large bowl, combine the beans with the chopped onions and green pepper. Pour the heated dressing over the beans and toss lightly to mix. Cover with plastic wrap and refrigerate overnight.

To serve, toss salad again and transfer to a fresh bowl using a slotted spoon to carry as little of the dressing over as possible. (Reserve the dressing to store any leftover beans; they will keep in the refrigerator for several days.)

*Transvaal*

# Brown Rice & Lentils

Serves 4–6
Often served hot as a side dish to meat, Brown Rice & Lentils also makes a filling salad when eaten cold. A green leaf salad goes well with it.

*250 ml (1 cup) brown rice*
*250 ml (1 cup) brown lentils*
*5 medium onions*
*Cooking oil*
*15 ml (1T) lemon juice*

Cook rice and lentils together in 1 to 1½ litres water with salt to taste; they will be tender after 30–45 minutes.

Chop the onions and cook gently in heated cooking oil until transparent (do not allow to brown). Add the rice and lentils to the saucepan and toss well. Add the lemon juice. (You could also add freshly ground black pepper, and crisp, chopped green pepper would be tasty and a contrast in textures if you are serving this as a salad.)

*Transvaal*

## Sweet & Sour Cucumbers

Makes 2 large jars
Sweet pickled cucumber slices to keep on hand for a salad accompaniment to cold meats or braai. (Slaked lime may be bought from the chemist.)

*3 English cucumbers, peeled & sliced*
*Lime water (5 ml slaked lime to 1 litre water)*

SYRUP
*375 ml (1½ cups) sugar*
*375 ml (1½ cups) vinegar*
*375 ml (1½ cups) water*
*8 whole allspice*
*10 peppercorns*
*5 cloves*
*15 ml (1T) caraway or dill seeds*
*Cinnamon stick (5 cm)*

Cover the cucumber slices, which should be about 1 cm thick, in lime water to cover, and allow to stand overnight. Drain, rinse off lime water and drain cucumber well again.

Mix the sugar with the vinegar, water and spices. Heat, stirring to dissolve the sugar. Bring to the boil and add the cucumber slices. Cook over low heat until slices are slightly transparent (about 10–15 minutes). Bottle in hot, sterilised jars (2 × 750 ml size) and store for 6 to 8 weeks before using. Once opened, keep in the refrigerator.

*Western Cape*

## Pickled Mushrooms

Serves 4–6
These lightly pickled mushrooms cooked Greek style are a tasty salad dish for lunchtime or a braai.

*500 g button mushrooms*
*1 small onion, chopped*
*1 clove garlic, crushed*
*125 ml (1/2 cup) olive oil*
*45 ml (3T) white wine*
*45 ml (3T) white vinegar*
*45 ml (3T) lemon juice*
*30 ml (2T) chopped chives*
*30 ml (2T) chopped parsley*
*2ml (1/2t) salt*
*Pinch cayenne pepper*

Wipe the mushrooms, which are to be left whole. Bring the remaining ingredients to the boil in a saucepan and add the mushrooms. Simmer for 5 minutes. Leave to cool overnight. Drain and serve, decorated with slices of lemon.

*Transvaal*

## Carrot & Banana Salad

Serves 6
A most pleasant variation on an old stand-by – and quick and easy to make.

*1 bunch medium carrots*
*2 ripe bananas*
*Juice of 2 oranges*

Scrape carrots and wash well. Grate into a large bowl (you can use the food processor for this). Peel and mash the bananas, and add to the grated carrots. Add the orange juice and mix until all is evenly distributed. Serve in a salad bowl lined with lettuce leaves.

*Western Cape*

# Pretty Pear Salad

Serves 2
An attractive light luncheon dish for a hot day.

*1 large, ripe pear*
*Lemon juice*
*Cooked rice*
*Lettuce leaves or shredded cabbage*
*Celery leaves (optional)*
*Spring onions or chives*
*2 small tomatoes*
*Salt & freshly ground black pepper*
*Cottage cheese of your choice*
*Slice cooked ham*
*10 ml (2t) mayonnaise*
*Cayenne pepper*

Peel the pear and cut it in half lengthwise, carefully removing the core. Place in a dish and sprinkle with lemon juice; turn in juice to prevent the pear discolouring.

On each serving plate, fill the centre with a few spoonfuls cooked rice; arrange the lettuce or cabbage and the celery leaves round the rice. Snip the spring onions or chives over the lettuce and add quarters of ripe tomato (these may be sprinkled with a little sugar beforehand if desired). Season with salt and pepper to taste.

Place each pear half cut side up on the bed of rice, using any leftover lemon/pear juice to sprinkle over the lettuce. Pile cottage cheese on the pear halves, sprinkle with chopped ham and top with mayonnaise. Finally sprinkle the pear with a little cayenne pepper for taste and colouring.

*Eastern Cape*

# Tuna & Smoked Mussel Salad

Serves 6
A rich meal-in-a-salad to be served with lemon wedges and homemade wholewheat bread.

*1 small lettuce*
*3 medium tomatoes, peeled & diced*
*250 ml (1 cup) cucumber, diced*
*6 radishes, thinly sliced*
*1 × 290g can asparagus tips, drained*
*1 × 200g can light meat tuna in oil*
*2 × 105g cans smoked mussels*
*3 hardboiled eggs halved*
*Half an onion, sliced thinly*
*Lemon wedges to serve*

DRESSING
*125 ml (1/2 cup) salad oil*
*(OR use oil drained from the tuna & mussels)*
*45 ml (3T) wine vinegar*
*2 ml (1/2t) salt*
*2 ml (1/2t) mustard powder*
*5 ml (1t) castor sugar*
*Freshly ground black pepper to taste*
*45 ml (3T) fresh parsley, chopped*

Shred the lettuce into a bowl or onto a serving platter. Combine dressing ingredients in a glass jar and shake well to combine. Scatter the tomato, cucumber, radishes and asparagus tips over the lettuce. Pour about two-thirds of the dressing over and toss very lightly.

Flake the tuna and scatter over the salad with the smoked mussels. Top with the remaining dressing. Arrange the halved hardboiled eggs round the rim of the bowl and scatter the onion rings in the centre.

Serve immediately with homemade bread, lemon wedges to squeeze over each serving (this is a rich salad), and chilled white wine.

*Western Cape*

# Grape & Cheese Salad

Serves 4–6
Green salad with grapes, cheese, nuts and crunchy croûtons for contrast.

*1 lettuce*
*150 g blackgrapes*
*150 g green grapes*
*125 g cheddar cheese*
*40 g chopped walnuts or pecan nuts*
*4 slices white bread, crusts removed*
*1 clove garlic, chopped or crushed*
*30 ml (2T) butter*

DRESSING
*50 ml salad oil*
*15 ml (1T) lemon juice*
*5 ml (1t) mustard powder*
*5 ml (1t) salt*

Wash and dry the lettuce, tearing the leaves into bite-size pieces and placing in a salad bowl. Halve the grapes, removing the seeds. Cut the cheddar cheese into strips. Combine grapes, cheese and chopped nuts with the lettuce. Mix the ingredients for the dressing in a screw-top bottle; shake well to combine and pour over the salad. Toss lightly.

Cut the bread into cubes. Heat the butter in a skillet and add garlic and the bread cubes: fry until they are crisp and golden. Sprinkle the croûtons over the salad, toss again lightly, and serve at once.

*Eastern Cape*

# Curried Chicken & Fruit Salad

Serves 4
A light meal that could be served on individual beds of lettuce.

*2 chicken breasts (cooked)*
*1 Granny Smith apple, diced*
*1 clingstone peach, diced*
*1 pear, diced*
*1 banana, sliced*
*180 ml (2/3 cup) mayonnaise*
*5 ml (1t) curry powder*

Cube the cooked chicken breasts and prepare the fruits (only the banana should be peeled). Mix the mayonnaise and curry powder and add to the chicken and fruit, coating the pieces.

*Transvaal*

# Old Fashioned Potato Salad

Serves 6
Traditional potato salad is a firm South African favourite
– this one has the surprise flavour of mint.

*1 kg potatoes*
*250 ml (1 cup) fresh mint, chopped*
*15 ml (1T) vinegar*
*1 large onion, chopped finely*
*500 ml (2 cups) thin cream (or more to taste)*
*Salt & freshly ground black pepper to taste*
*3 hardboiled eggs, chopped, for garnish*
*1 red pepper, sliced thinly (optional)*

Scrub the potatoes and steam them in their skins. Steep
the chopped mint in the vinegar. Drain mint and add,
with the onion, to the cream (the richness will be
tempered by the onion and vinegar-soaked mint). Add
salt and pepper to taste and mix well.

Peel the still-warm potatoes and slice evenly but
quickly – they must not be cool when you pour the
cream dressing over, tossing lightly to coat all the potato
evenly. Leave the bowl in a cool place to allow the
potato to absorb the cream; this will take 3–4 hours.
Cover and chill overnight. Serve in a pretty glass bowl
and garnish with the chopped egg and strips of red
pepper for contrast.

*Transvaal*

# Summer Rice Salad

Serves 4–6
A salad that keeps well when made ahead, and can be
made with white rice or nutty brown rice.

*500 ml (2 cups) cooked rice*
*1 × 410 g can sliced peaches, drained & cubed*
*4–5 bananas, sliced & sprinkled with lemon juice*
*250–500 ml (1–2 cups) celery, chopped*
*125 ml (1/2 cup) red or green pepper, chopped*
*1/2 onion, chopped finely*
*125 ml (1/2 cup) fresh parsley, chopped*
*125 ml (1/2 cup) seedless raisins*
*125 ml (1/2 cup) sunflower seeds*

DRESSING
*125 ml (1/2 cup) sunflower oil*
*10 ml (2t) lemon juice*
*10 ml (2t) curry powder*
*15 ml (1T) soya sauce*
*15 ml (1T) honey*

Prepare salad ingredients and mix gently in a large
bowl. Combine dressing ingredients and shake well;
pour over the salad, toss to mix, and allow to stand for
about 6 hours, covered, in the refrigerator. (Stores well
in a sealed container.)

*Transvaal*

# Butternut Salad

Serves 4
A very unusual salad with a fresh, different flavour.

*Half a butternut squash*
*2 Granny Smith apples*
*6–8 granadillas, or 1/2 can granadilla pulp*

Peel and grate the squash into a bowl. Grate the unpeeled apples into the bowl. Mix the fruit and squash with the pulp of the granadillas. Chill before serving.

*Eastern Cape*

# Potato Skin Salad

Serves 4–6
Leftover baked potatoes from a braai are used skin and all in this economical and quite delicious salad.

*4 large cooked potatoes*
*100 ml finely chopped garlic chives*
*250 ml (1 cup) mayonnaise, preferably homemade*
*Fresh parsley, chopped*
*Sesame seeds for garnish*

Use any leftover (even overcooked) potatoes, so long as the flesh has not turned brown. Place in a low oven (140 °C) for about 1 hour. Chop into small pieces, skin and all. Add the garlic chives and the mayonnaise (a good bought variety will do). Mix gently, sprinkle with parsley and sesame seeds, and chill before serving.

*Transvaal*

*Opposite:* Pea & Bacon Salad, a winning combination of tastes and textures
*Overleaf:* Seasonal Salad with Blaauwkrantz Balls, an eye-catching salad that is also ideal for vegetarians
*Prepared with choice ingredients from Woolworths food markets*

# Fish & Seafood

# Fish & Seafood

### Hot Fish Dishes
Fish Fillets in Sour Cream, 50
Fish Fillets in Tomato Cream Sauce, 40
Fish Goulash, 39
Fish Lasagne, 54
Fish Plait, 53
Mock Cape Thermidor, 51
Quick Smoked Haddock Casserole, 44
Smoked Snoek & Potato Casserole, 49
Snoek, Smoked Angelfish & Mussel Stew, 49
Soufflé Kingklip Pie, 44
Spiced Blue Fish, 52
Tropical Fried Fish, 39
Tunny with Anchovies, 50

### Cold Fish Dishes
Cold Lemon Tunny, 53
Fish Vinaigrette, 41
Pickled Fish, 40
Spinach Salmon Roulade, 43

### Seafood
Baked Rock Lobster Tails & Avocado, 42
Black Mussels off the Rocks, 52
Seafood Risotto, 51
Simon's Town Calamari, 42
Creamed Oysters or Mussels on Wholewheat Toast, 43

# Tropical Fried Fish

(Illustrated on page 45)

Serves 4

A tropical blend of fruit, coconut and fish. Use firm white fish such as kingklip, kabeljou or Cape salmon.

*4 large fillets of white fish*
*30 ml (1T) soy sauce or garam masala*
*Freshly ground black pepper*
*Seasoned salt*
*Flour*
*2 eggs, beaten*
*250 ml (1 cup) desiccated coconut*
*150 ml white bread crumbs*
*Oil for frying*
*250 ml (1 cup) seedless grapes, peeled*
*8 prunes, soaked in 50 ml brandy*
*2 bananas, sliced*

Sprinkle the fish fillets with the soy sauce or the garam masala (a spicy curry mix) and seasoning. Roll the fillets in flour, dip in beaten egg and lastly roll in the coconut and breadcrumbs mixed. Press this coating lightly; leaving the prepared fillets in the refrigerator until needed is also a good idea to firm them.

Heat the oil in a frying pan and fry the fillets for about 6–8 minutes on each side. Remove from pan and keep hot. Using a fresh pan, sauté the fruit in a little oil for a few minutes only. Serve fish and fruit on a bed of rice, with a fresh green salad.

*Eastern Cape*

# Fish Goulash

Serves 6

A delightfully different idea for a fish dish, easily prepared and ideal for dinner parties. Use any firm white fish, preferably avoiding hake – fresh angelfish or kingklip is a good choice.

*1,5 kg firm fish, filleted*
*250 g streaky bacon*
*2 large onions, sliced into rings*
*1 chicken stock cube, crumbled*
*500 ml (2 cups) sour cream/Smetena*
*4 tomatoes, skinned, or 410 g can peeled tomatoes*
*Salt & black pepper to taste*
*5 ml (1t) paprika*
*5 ml (1t) sugar*
*Juice of 1 lemon*
*Grated rind of 1 lemon*
*250 g black mushrooms, sliced*
*30 ml (2T) cornflour mixed with a little water*
*Chopped chives or celery leaves for garnish*

Cut the fish into bite-sized pieces. Dice the bacon and fry in a large saucepan; add the onion rings and sauté until transparent. Add the fish pieces, plus the stock cube, sour cream, tomato, seasonings, lemon juice and rind. Stir gently to mix, cover and simmer very gently for 30 minutes. Add the sliced mushroom and simmer for another 15 minutes. Add the cornflour and cook for 10 minutes, stirring occasionally, to thicken sauce. Serve on a bed of brown rice, and garnish with the chives or celery leaves. A green salad is a good accompaniment.

*Western Cape*

## Pickled Fish

Makes about 28 portions
A Cape favourite made with a firm fish such as kabeljou or yellowtail; hake may tend to fall apart as it is less firm.

*7 kg fresh, firm fish, filleted*
*Salt & pepper to taste*
*Flour for dredging fish*
*Cooking oil to fry fish*

VINEGAR MIXTURE
*5 large onions, sliced into thin rings*
*Oil for frying*
*15 ml (1T) strong curry powder*
*1 litre vinegar*
*30 ml (2T) sugar (or diabetic jam)*
*30 ml (2T) turmeric*
*15 ml (1T) cornflour*
*5 ml (1t) salt*
*2 ml (1/2t) pepper*

Cut fish into neat pieces, season with salt and pepper, dredge lightly with flour, and fry until golden. (You may also steam the pieces until cooked.)

TO MAKE VINEGAR MIXTURE: In a large saucepan, sauté the onion rings lightly in a little oil; add the curry powder and fry for a few minutes more. Mix the vinegar with the sugar, turmeric, cornflour and salt and pepper and stir into the onions. Simmer gently for 5 minutes. Set aside to cool.

Pack the fried fish in glass bottles (you may add a bay leaf and extra onion to each bottle). Pour over the cooled vinegar mixture, seal and store for 2 days before using.

This fish, covered, will keep for a month in the refrigerator. Serve with a salad and fresh bread and butter.

*Garden Route, Cape*

## Fish Fillets in Tomato Cream Sauce

Serves 4
Use fresh, firm fillets of white fish (such as kingklip or kabeljou). Be careful not to use wine that is too dry and harsh.

*1 kg fish fillets*
*Freshly ground black pepper*
*Seasoning salt*
*1 medium onion, chopped*
*Oil and butter for sautéing onion*
*1 × 400 g can peeled tomatoes, drained*
*125 ml (1/2 cup) dry white wine*
*2 ml (1/2t) sugar*
*30 ml (2T) parsley, chopped*
*250 ml (1 cup) cream*

Season the fish fillets with freshly ground black pepper and one of the flavoured salts available. Heat a little oil and butter mixed in a large frying pan, and sauté the onion gently until soft. Chop the drained tomatoes (you may keep the juice for some other purpose), and stir them into the onion with the wine, sugar and parsley. Bring to the boil and add the fish fillets, then simmer gently for about 8 minutes until the fish is done but not overcooked.

Use a slotted spoon to transfer fish to a warm serving dish, and keep warm while you reduce the sauce: boil the liquid in the pan until it is reduced by half and has thickened. Stir in the cream and cook a little longer (but do not allow to boil). Check the sauce for seasoning – you may need extra black pepper and salt. Pour the sauce over the fish. Serve at once with rice, baby green beans or a salad, and a crisp white wine.

*Transvaal*

# Fish Vinaigrette

Serves 6
A delicious cold dish for a hot summer's day – use a firm white fish such as Cape salmon, kabeljou, white steenbras or white stumpnose. Save the head and trimmings to make the stock.

*1,5 kg fresh fish, filleted*

FISH STOCK
*Fish head & trimmings*
*1 onion, sliced thinly*
*1 carrot, diced*
*1 stalk celery, chopped*
*Sprig of parsley*
*1 fresh bayleaf or lemon leaf*
*4 whole peppercorns*
*Few strips lemon rind*
*250 ml (1 cup) water*
*250 ml (1 cup) white wine*

VINAIGRETTE
*Juice of 1 lemon*
*10 ml (2t) white vinegar*
*5 ml (1t) castor sugar*
*5 ml (1t) French mustard*
*Salt & freshly ground black pepper*
*15 ml (1T) fresh parsley, chopped*
*125 ml (1/2 cup) olive & sunflower oil, mixed*

GARNISH
*175 g Danish herring*
*175 g fresh mussels, steamed (or canned mussels in shells)*
*1 sweet red pepper, blanched & sliced thinly*
*Spring onions, sliced thinly*
*350 g black olives*

Cut the fish fillets into bite size pieces or into strips.

FOR THE STOCK: Place all stock ingredients in a saucepan, bring to the boil and then simmer for 30 minutes. Strain, reserving the liquid. Pour the stock into a large, shallow frying pan and bring to the boil. Add the fish fillets a few at a time, reducing heat to a very gentle simmer to poach them until just cooked through (do not overcook). Remove fillets with a slotted spoon and keep aside in a serving dish.

FOR VINAIGRETTE: Combine all the vinaigrette ingredients, whisking until emulsified and creamy. Pour over the still warm fillets to coat well. (The remaining poaching stock can be reduced by half by boiling rapidly, and added to the vinaigrette to extend it.)

TO GARNISH: Slice the herring in small strips and arrange over the fillets. Scatter with the mussels, the sliced red pepper (do not use the seeds), the spring onion and the olives.

Leave to stand for a while before serving, and baste occasionally with the vinaigrette. Serve at room temperature – delicious with boiled whole baby potatoes and a simple mixed green leaf salad.

*Western Cape*

## Baked Rock Lobster Tails & Avocado

(Illustrated on front cover)

Serves 3 (or 6 as starter)

Rock lobster (crayfish) tails are sold at good super-markets and are better value than whole lobster. A lavish recipe for special occasions – it can be prepared ahead up to the final stage before baking, and stored covered in the refrigerator until needed.

*4 lobster tails*
*3 avocados*
*Lemon juice*
*1 large onion, chopped*
*1 green pepper, chopped*
*50 g butter*
*125 g black mushrooms, sliced*
*250 ml (1 cup) cream*
*Salt & black pepper to taste*
*Cheddar cheese, finely grated*
*Fresh breadcrumbs*
*Paprika*

Cook the lobster tails according to instructions, remove flesh and dice. Cut the avocado pears in half and brush well with lemon juice to avoid discolouring. Sauté the onion and green pepper in the butter until golden. Add the sliced mushrooms and cook for 5 minutes. Add the diced lobster and the cream, season with salt and freshly ground black pepper to taste, and stir until nicely thickened.

Spoon the mixture into the avocado halves, and sprinkle with grated cheese and breadcrumbs, and paprika for colour. Place in a shallow pan with 2 cm hot water. Bake in oven preheated to 180 °C for 20 minutes. Serve with a good mixed salad.

*Swaziland*

## Simon's Town Calamari

Serves 4

Squid or calamari need not always be deep fried in rings – in this tasty dish, the tubes are stuffed and served with a sauce. Use fresh squid if you are lucky enough to find them available.

*400 g frozen calamari tubes*
*1 small onion, finely chopped*
*100 g mushrooms, chopped*
*Butter*
*250 g chunky cottage cheese*
*10 ml (2t) fresh parsley, chopped*
*2 ml (1/2t) dried thyme*
*Salt & black pepper to taste*
*200 ml dry white wine*
*250 ml (1 cup) sour cream/Smetena*
*1 egg yolk, beaten*
*Salt & black pepper to taste*
*Chopped parsley to garnish*

Pour boiling water over the frozen calamari tubes and leave to thaw for 5 minutes.

Sauté the onion and mushrooms in a little butter. Add to the cottage cheese with the herbs and seasoning to taste; mix together and pour off any excess liquid. Use this mixture to stuff the calamari tubes. Place in an ovenproof dish.

In a saucepan, heat the wine and the sour cream but do not boil. Pour the mixture over the beaten egg yolk and stir well. Return mixture to the saucepan and stir over gentle heat until slightly thickened. Do NOT allow to boil. Taste for seasoning. Pour over the stuffed cala-mari tubes and bake at 160 °C for 20–30 minutes. If the liquid is too runny, thicken with a little cornflour and water mixed.

Garnish with fresh chopped parsley. Serve with rice and a green salad.

*Western Cape*

## Creamed Oysters or Mussels on Wholewheat Toast

Serves 4

A tasty emergency dish from the store cupboard to serve as a starter or a light supper dish. If you have a smoke-box, you might smoke your own mussels or oysters for this dish.

*1 × 105 g can smoked oysters or mussels*
*4 slices wholewheat toast, buttered*
*30 ml (2T) spring onions, finely chopped*
*30 ml (2T) dry white wine*
*125 ml (1/2 cup) cream*
*15 ml (1T) fresh parsley, chopped*
*Dash of lemon juice*
*Salt & white pepper to taste*

Drain the oysters, reserving the liquid from the can. Butter the toast and keep warm. Combine spring onions with wine in a saucepan and cook over medium heat for a few minutes to reduce the wine. Add 30 ml (2T) of the oyster liquid and the cream and cook again, stirring constantly to reduce (do NOT allow to boil). Add the oysters and simmer for 3 minutes to warm oysters through. Stir in chopped parsley, a dash of lemon juice, and salt and pepper to taste. Spoon over the hot buttered toast and serve immediately.

*Eastern Cape*

## Spinach Salmon Roulade

Serves 6

An excellent light meal, equally good served hot or cold.

SALMON FILLING
*2 × 200 g cans pink salmon*
*60 ml (4T) onion, chopped finely*
*125 ml (1/2 cup) mayonnaise*
*Black pepper to taste*

ROULADE
*250 g frozen chopped spinach*
*60 g butter*
*75 ml flour*
*250 ml (1 cup) milk*
*5 ml (1t) salt*
*4 eggs, separated*

FILLING: Drain the salmon, skinning and deboning it. Mix with the onion, mayonnaise and black pepper; set aside.

Cook the frozen spinach over medium heat until all the liquid evaporates; keep on one side. In another saucepan, make a white sauce by melting the butter, stirring in the flour and adding the milk slowly; stir over medium heat, bringing to the boil and stirring continuously until the sauce thickens. Add the salt.

Cool the sauce, then add the 4 egg yolks to the sauce one at a time, beating well after each addition. Add the spinach. Now beat the 4 egg whites until standing in stiff peaks, and fold carefully into the spinach mix.

Grease a Swiss roll tin (25 cm × 30 cm), cover the base with greaseproof paper and grease the paper itself with butter or magarine. Now pour the spinach mix into the Swiss roll tin and spread carefully. Bake in oven preheated to 200 °C for 12–15 minutes. Turn out onto a damp towel and gently remove lining paper.

Spread the roll with the salmon filling. Using the damp towel to assist, roll the roulade lengthwise gently. Ease onto a serving platter and garnish with with sprigs of fresh dill or fennel.

*Transvaal*

# Quick Smoked Haddock Casserole

Serves 6
A simple dish for brunch or Sunday supper.

*1 kg smoked haddock, cut in bite size pieces*
*500 g new potatoes, boiled & peeled*
*250 ml (1 cup) milk*
*30 ml (2T) butter*
*1 egg yolk*
*5 ml (1t) cornflour*
*1 ml (1/4t) freshly ground coriander*
*2 ml (1/2t) curry powder*
*Freshly ground black pepper to taste*
*125 g mushrooms, sliced*
*30 ml (2T) spring onion, chopped*
*125 ml (1/2 cup) cream*
*Chopped parsley to garnish*

Place haddock, potatoes, milk and butter in a large pot and simmer for 5 minutes. Remove haddock and potatoes to a heated dish and keep warm. Beat the egg yolk and cornflour with a fork. Add a little of the hot milk and blend. Pour the egg mixture into the pot, add spices and seasoning, sliced mushrooms, spring onion and cream. Cook gently for 8 minutes or so, stirring sauce with a wooden spoon until it thickens (do not allow to boil). Pour the sauce over the haddock and potatoes, and garnish with the parsley. Serve with crusty rolls and a green salad.

*Transvaal*

*Opposite:* Tropical Fried Fish, a prizewinner that blends fruit, coconut and fish
*Overleaf: (left)* Sesame Noodle Salad; and *(right)* Mushroom Quiche with Waterblommetjies, a delicately flavoured treat for outdoor eating
*Page 48:* Stuffed Flat-Chicken Potjie, cooked over the coals
*Prepared with choice ingredients from Woolworths food markets*

# Soufflé Kingklip Pie

Serves 4
An unusual fish soufflé-cum-pie to serve as a light lunch or supper dish with salad and fresh crusty rolls or wholewheat bread.

*500 g kingklip fillets*
*200 ml water*
*1 bayleaf*
*3 peppercorns*
*1 clove*
*1 small onion, finely chopped*
*Milk*
*50 g butter*
*50 g flour*
*5 ml (1t) anchovy paste*
*Salt & pepper to taste*
*15 ml (1T) finely chopped fresh parsley*
*1 egg, separated*
*2 ml (1/2t) prepared mustard*
*60 g cheddar cheese, grated*
*1 extra egg white*

Cook the fish gently in the water with the bayleaf, peppercorns, clove and onion for 10 minutes. Remove the fish (reserving the liquid) and skin and debone it, flaking the flesh. Strain the liquid and make up to 375 ml with milk. Melt the butter in a saucepan, add the flour and stir over heat; add the anchovy paste and the "fishy" milk and stir to make a sauce, cooking this until it is thick and smooth. Remove from heat. Put half the sauce into a bowl, add salt and pepper to taste, the chopped parsley and the flaked kingklip, mixing well; put into a greased soufflé dish.

Stir the egg yolk, mustard and grated cheese into the remaining sauce in the saucepan. Whisk the egg white and extra egg white until soft peaks are formed, then fold carefully into the sauce in the saucepan. Now spread this soufflé mixture on top of the fish mixture. Bake in oven preheated to 200 °C for 25–30 minutes. Serve immediately with a salad.

*Transvaal*

# Smoked Snoek & Potato Casserole

Serves 6
Try smoked angelfish for a variation of this casserole, which is a different approach to "smoored" snoek. The dish can be made ahead, and also freezes well.

*1 kg smoked snoek*
*4 large tomatoes, skinned & sliced*
*1 onion, thinly sliced into rings*
*6 large potatoes, boiled, skinned & sliced*
*125 g cheddar cheese, grated*
*250 ml (1 cup) cream*
*Salt & pepper to taste*
*15 ml (1T) Parmesan cheese, finely grated*
*125 ml (1/2 cup) fresh white breadcrumbs*
*15 ml (1T) finely chopped fresh parsley to garnish*

Skin and debone the smoked snoek carefully; flake the fish. Lightly grease a deep ovenproof casserole dish and place a layer of the flaked fish in the base. Cover with a layer of tomato slices and onion rings, then a layer of sliced potato, and sprinkle with a little of the grated cheddar cheese. Repeat layers until the ingredients have been used up, ending with a layer of potatoes.

Mix the cream with salt and pepper to taste and pour over the layers. Combine the remaining cheddar cheese with the Parmesan cheese and bread crumbs and scatter over the top of the casserole. Place on a baking tray and bake in an oven preheated to 180 °C for about 30 minutes, or until topping is golden brown and crisp. Sprinkle with chopped parsley and serve hot, with a salad on the side.

*Western Cape*

# Snoek, Smoked Angelfish & Mussel Stew

Serves 2-4
A different fish dish that is especially useful for up-country, where the range of fresh fish is limited.

*200 g smoked snoek*
*100 g smoked angelfish*
*1 × 105 g can smoked mussels*
*45 ml (3T) butter*
*1 large onion, chopped*
*2 large cloves garlic, crushed*
*1 medium aubergine/brinjal, peeled and cubed*
*1 × 400 g can peeled tomatoes, chopped roughly (use juice)*
*15 ml (1T) tomato puree*
*Few drops Tabasco sauce*
*Salt & freshly ground black pepper to taste*

Cut the snoek into bite-sized pieces, discarding bones. Debone and flake the smoked angelfish. Drain the smoked mussels.

Melt the butter in a saucepan and sauté the onion and garlic until just transparent. Add the cubed aubergine and fry for 2–3 minutes before adding the rest of the ingredients – but add the prepared snoek, angelfish and mussels last, or they may break up in the mixing.

Cover and simmer for about 30 minutes. Check seasoning. Serve on a bed of rice – fresh herbs or parsley would make a good garnish, and a green salad goes well on the side.

*Orange Free State*

# Tunny with Anchovies

Serves 4–6

Marinated tunny (tuna) steaks stuffed with anchovies are served with anchovy bread for extra emphasis.

*1 kg tunny cut into 2,5 cm steaks*
*1 × 56 g can anchovies, drained*
*Salt & black pepper to taste*
*250 ml (1 cup) cooking oil*
*5 ml (1t) dried mixed herbs*
*Juice of 1 lemon*
*250 g tomatoes, peeled*
*2 medium onions, grated*
*1 small green pepper, chopped*
*2 cloves garlic, crushed*
*250 ml (1 cup) white wine*

Cut two crosswise slits in each slice of tunny and stuff with anchovies.

Salt and pepper the steaks well, to taste. Blend three-quarters of the oil with the mixed herbs and the lemon juice and pour over the tunny steaks. Leave to marinate for 1 hour. Heat the remaining oil in a pan and fry the whole, peeled tomatoes, the onion, green pepper and garlic gently until soft. When the mixture is fairly thick, add the wine. Place the tunny steaks on top of the mixture, cover and cook slowly for about 20–25 minutes.

When the steaks are cooked through, remove them to a warmed serving dish and keep hot. Rub the tomato mixture through a sieve or puree in a blender, and pour over the tunny steaks.

Serve with rice and salad, and an anchovy-buttered French loaf made in the following way: Mash a small can of drained anchovies with 125 g butter or margarine, slice the French loaf leaving the bottom crust intact, and spread with the anchovy butter. Wrap the loaf in foil and bake at 180 °C for 20 minutes or until heated through.

*Western Cape*

# Fish Fillets in Sour Cream

Serves 4

A lemony sour cream sauce lifts even frozen fish fillets from the ordinary. Use kingklip or good hake.

*750 g firm white fish, filleted*
*1 large onion, chopped*
*45 ml (3T) butter*
*20 ml (4t) lemon juice*
*375 ml sour cream/Smetena*
*5 ml (1t) salt*
*Pepper to taste*
*2 ml (1/2t) paprika*
*2 egg yolks, beaten*
*2 ml (1/2t) dried basil (or 5 ml fresh basil, chopped)*

Cut the fillets into bite-sized pieces. In a large frying pan, sauté the onion in the butter until golden, then add the lemon juice, sour cream, salt, pepper to taste and paprika. Heat to just below boiling, but do not boil; add the pieces of fish gradually so as not to lower the heat too much. Finally simmer the fish gently for 10 minutes. Remove the fish with a slotted spoon and place in a warmed serving dish; keep warm. Pour some of the cream mixture over the beaten egg yolks and return to the pan, cooking the sauce over low heat until it thickens. Add the basil and test for seasoning. Pour the sauce over the fish and serve immediately with rice or mashed potatoes, baby carrots and peas.

*Natal*

# Seafood Risotto

Serves 4
An extravagant risotto for special evenings.

*2 rock lobster tails, cooked*
*200 g kingklip fillet, steamed*
*1 × 200 g can of salmon*
*500 g king prawns, cooked*
*1 × 825 g can mussels on the shell*
*500 ml (2 cups) white rice, cooked until fluffy*
*100 g pecan nuts*
*100 g cashew nuts*

TOMATO MIXTURE
*2 large tomatoes*
*30 ml (2T) tomato paste*
*60 ml (4T) cooking oil*
*3 onions, sliced thinly*
*3 cloves garlic, crushed*
*1 large red pepper, cut into thin strips*
*5 ml (1t) paprika*
*2 ml (1/2 t) turmeric*
*10 ml (2t) sugar*
*Salt & black pepper to taste*

GARNISH
*Spring onions or chives, chopped finely*
*Sprigs of fresh parsley*
*Lemon slices or wedges*

Prepare the seafood, cutting the rock lobster and fish into bite size pieces, and draining the salmon; place together in a large bowl. (The cooked prawns and the drained mussels should be kept on one side for the moment.) Add the cooked rice and the nuts.

FOR THE TOMATO MIXTURE: Peel and puree the tomatoes, adding the tomato paste. Heat the oil in a saucepan and sauté the onion, garlic and red pepper until softened. Sprinkle over the paprika, turmeric and sugar, add the tomato puree/paste and cook for 5 minutes. Add salt and pepper to taste, and fold mixture gently into the seafood-rice mix, being careful to blend the flavours without breaking up the seafood.

Turn the mixture into an ovenproof dish and lay the cooked prawns and drained mussels on top. Cover and heat in a moderate (180 °C) oven, but do not allow to bake or dry out. Remove from oven, sprinkle with chives or spring onions and decorate with the parsley and lemon. Serve with salad and a good wine of your choice.

*Natal*

# Mock Cape Thermidor

Serves 4 (or 6 as starter)
If your budget allows, you can replace the fish with the real thing – Cape rock lobster (crayfish). An excellent recipe.

*1 kg monkfish, cooked & cut in bite size pieces*
*15 ml (1T) butter*
*1 medium onion, chopped*
*300 g button mushrooms, sliced and salted*
*5 ml (1t) parsley, chopped*
*2 ml (1/2t) ground black peppercorns*
*250 ml (1 cup) cream*
*50 ml sherry*
*150 ml white wine*
*15 ml (1T) French or country mustard*
*15 ml (1T) tomato paste*
*375 ml (1½ cups) mature cheddar cheese, grated*
*Puff pastry (homemade or bought)*

Place cooked monkfish in a casserole dish. In a heavy-based saucepan, melt butter and lightly sauté onion. Add the mushrooms and sauté for another minute or two. Add parsley and peppercorns and simmer. Add cream, sherry, wine, mustard and tomato paste. Mix well and allow to thicken on low heat. (If the sauce remains too runny, you can thicken it with a little cornflour; however, the mustard and tomato paste should thicken it sufficiently.)

Add cheese and pour the mixture over the fish. Cover the dish with the pastry and bake in 180 °C oven until pastry is cooked. (Mashed potato is an alternative topping.) Serve with rice and fresh seasonal vegetables.

*Natal*

## Spiced Blue Fish

Serves 4–6

If blue fish (a deep-sea fish) is not available, use any fresh, firm white fish which does not tend to disintegrate. The fruit juice must not contain added sugar. The dish is very fiery and Oriental – for milder palates substitute a dash of Tabasco, a clove of garlic (crushed) and a teaspoon of paprika for the garlic-chilli sauce.

*1 kg fresh blue fish, filleted*
*200 ml orange-mango or orange-peach juice*
*200 ml dry white wine*
*30 ml (2T) garlic-chilli sauce*
*20 ml (4t) hot lime or mango pickle/atjar*
*10 ml (2t) salt*
*2 ml (1/2t) freshly ground black pepper*
*2 large onions, sliced very thinly*
*1 large green pepper, sliced into thin rings*
*12 baby carrots, cut into julienne strips*
*100 g red cabbage, sliced very thinly*

Preheat oven to 160 °C. Place the fish fillets in an ovenproof dish and pour over the fruit juice and wine mixed with the garlic-chilli sauce, lime pickle, salt and black pepper. This should cover the fish. Strew the vegetables over the fish, reserving half the red cabbage for later. Cover and bake in the oven for 30–45 minutes, or until cooked through.

Five minutes before the end of baking, add the remaining red cabbage (this is to enhance the colour scheme). Serve hot with saffron rice and sambals, or allow to cool and serve cold in the style of pickled fish.

*Western Cape*

## Black Mussels off the Rocks

Serves 2–4

For those fortunate enough to be able to collect their own black mussels (remember each adult in a party may only collect 25). If you have a herb garden, fresh origanum or marjoram is a refreshing alternative to the parsley – use half the amount, as the flavour is more potent.

*50 black mussels*
*1 large onion, chopped*
*2 cloves garlic, crushed*
*60 ml (4T) butter*
*1 stalk celery, chopped finely*
*500 ml (2 cups) dry white wine*
*125 ml (1/2 cup) water*
*30 ml (2T) lemon juice*
*60 ml (4T) fresh parsley, finely chopped*
*Sprig of fresh thyme*
*1 bayleaf*
*Freshly ground black pepper to taste*
*30 ml (2T) butter, blended with 10 ml (2t) flour*
*Salt to taste*
*Extra chopped parsley for garnish*

Clean mussels thoroughly by scraping and rinsing under running water. (At this stage discard any mussels that are not tightly closed.) Leave for two hours in fresh water. Drain. In a deep pot, sauté the onion and garlic in the butter until golden. Add the celery and sauté. Then add the wine, water, lemon juice, parsley, thyme, bayleaf and black pepper to taste. Bring to the boil. Add the cleaned mussels, cover and boil rapidly until the mussels open (about 5 minutes), shaking the pot occasionally. Use slotted spoon to remove the opened mussels to a serving dish; keep warm. (At this stage, you should throw out any mussels that refuse to open.)

Add the butter/flour mixture to the liquid in the pot, whisking well to mix; cook for a few more minutes to thicken the sauce, testing for seasoning and adding salt to taste. Spoon the sauce over the mussels, sprinkle with a little extra chopped parsley and serve immediately, with fresh crusty bread to mop up the juices.

*Western Cape*

# Cold Lemon Tunny

Serves 4–6
Home-cooked tuna set in its own lemon-flavoured jelly makes a delicious summer meal.

*1 kg fresh tunny (tuna)*
*Lemon juice and white wine*
*1 litre water*
*1 onion, sliced*
*2 bayleaves or lemon leaves*
*Few peppercorns & allspice*
*5 ml (1t) salt*

Remove the skin and slice the tunny off the bones. Reserve the skin and bones for the stock (see below). Marinate the slices overnight in a mixture of lemon juice and white wine. (The fish will turn light pink in colour.) Make a stock of the water, onion, bayleaves, spices and salt boiled up with the bones and skin of the tunny for about 45 minutes. Strain, then use this strained stock mixed with the juices of the marinade to poach the slices of tunny gently, until the fish is just tender. (Do not overcook.)

Place the slices of fish on a serving dish and pour some of the stock and juice over; leave to cool. The juices should form an aspic. Serve chilled, with salads.

*Western Cape*

# Fish Plait

Serves 6
A recipe that makes a gourmet meal out of economical hake.

*500 g choice hake fillets*
*50 g button mushrooms*
*1 roll frozen puff pastry*
*50 g margarine or butter*
*50 g flour*
*200 ml milk mixed with 50 ml cream*
*Fresh parsley, finely chopped*
*Salt and freshly ground black pepper to taste*
*2 eggs, hard boiled and sliced*
*Beaten egg to brush pastry*
*Lemon slices or wedges for garnish*

Steam the hake until cooked, then flake gently. Set aside. Slice the mushrooms and cook in a little seasoned water until soft; drain and set aside. Set the pastry aside to thaw out. Meanwhile make a white sauce with the margarine, flour and milk/cream mixture and season it to taste, adding the parsley last. When thick, add the fish and mushrooms, folding them in gently off the heat.

Roll out the thawed puff pastry and trim to about 30 cm square. Lay the pastry in a greased baking tray, and spread the fish filling down the centre of the pastry, leaving a good margin on either side. Now cut the pastry on either side into narrow (15 mm) strips. Lay the slices of hard-boiled egg down the filling, brush the edges of the cut strips with beaten egg, and "plait" the strips, folding them alternately across the filling from either side, to give a plaited effect. When completed, brush over with beaten egg. Bake in an oven preheated to 200 °C for 30 minutes or until pastry is golden. Place on serving platter, decorate with lemon slices or wedges, and serve warm with a green salad.

*Transvaal*

# Fish Lasagne

Serves 6–8

A variation on a traditional dish, using tuna from the store cupboard.

*2 × 200 g cans light meat tuna*
*200 g green ribbon noodles*
*30 ml (2T) oil*
*4 medium onions, sliced*
*60 ml (4T) butter or margarine*
*1 × 425 g can tomato soup (or tomato puree)*
*100 ml water*
*Salt & freshly ground black pepper to taste*
*2 cloves garlic, crushed*
*5 ml (1t) dried origanum*
*2 × 250 g tubs chunky cottage cheese*
*250 ml (1 cup) grated cheddar cheese*
*250 ml (1 cup) cream*

Drain the oil or water from the tuna; set aside. Boil the noodles in salted water, adding the oil; when done, drain and keep aside. In a saucepan, sauté the onions in the butter until transparent; add the drained tuna, the tomato soup or puree, the water, seasonings, garlic and origanum; simmer for 10 minutes. Mix the cottage cheese, grated cheddar and cream together well, to form a sauce.

In a large, shallow ovenproof lasagne dish, arrange layers of noodles, tomato/fish mixture and cheese/cream sauce, in that order, repeating until ingredients are used up. Sprinkle extra grated cheddar cheese over and bake in oven preheated to 180 °C for about 20–25 minutes, to heat thoroughly and melt the cheese. Serve hot, with salad.

*Eastern Cape*

# Outdoor Cooking

# Outdoor Cooking

Avocado Quiche, 57
Baked Mealies & Tomatoes, 60
Bread Rolls with Chicken Liver Stuffing, 59
Fantan Rolls, 59
Maize Bread for the Braai, 58
Margie's Pumpkin, 60
Mealiemeal Muffins, 58
Mushroom Quiche with Waterblommetjies, 57
Sweetcorn Muffins, 58
Vegetable Potjiekos, 61

*Meat Dishes*
Beef Fillet-in-a-Loaf, 61
Mixed Kebabs for the Braai, 62
Oxtail Potjiekos, 63
Picnic Fillet of Beef, 60
Stuffed Flat-Chicken Potjie, 63
Venison Kebabs, 62
Venison Potjie Roast, 63
Wildevy Venison Potjiekos, 63

# Mushroom Quiche with Waterblommetjies

(Illustrated on page 47)

Serves 4–6

The delicate flavour of Cape waterblommetjies is preserved in this crustless quiche by using cultured buttermilk (yogurt would be too sour, but you could substitute 250 g smooth cottage cheese mixed with a little cream or milk to make 250 ml liquid). In Cape dishes sorrel ("suring") means the leaves of the yellow oxalis that blooms in autumn and winter.

*1 × 410 g can waterblommetjies, drained*
*100 g button mushrooms*
*1 large onion*
*30 ml (2T) cooking oil*
*15 ml (1T) sorrel, chopped (if available)*
*30 ml (2T) selfraising flour*
*250 ml (1 cup) cultured buttermilk*
*4 eggs, lightly beaten*
*2 ml (1/2t) celery salt*

TOPPING
*250 ml (1 cup) cheddar cheese, finely grated*
*15 ml (1T) Parmesan cheese*
*15 ml (1T) chopped fresh parsley*

Drain the canned waterblommetjies well in a colander. You could also use fresh waterblommetjies, washed well and blanched. Slice the mushrooms spherically, into medallions, and chop the onion finely. Pour the oil into a pan or wok suitable for stir-frying; add the mushrooms, onion and waterblommetjies, and the sorrel if available, and stir briskly over the heat for 2–3 minutes to allow the flavours to develop. Add the flour, stir well, then add the buttermilk and the lightly beaten eggs. Season with the celery salt. Stir and pour into a greased ovenproof glass dish (about 22 cm in diameter).

Preheat oven to 180 °C and bake the quiche for 30–35 minutes until set. About 10 minutes before the end of baking time, mix the cheese topping and sprinkle over the quiche, to allow the cheese to melt. Cool the quiche slightly before serving. (It is also excellent cold.)

If you would like the quiche to be more filling, you could use a shortcrust pastry base, semi baked in advance.

*Western Cape*

# Avocado Quiche

Serves 4–6

When avocados are plentiful, here is a different way to serve them – in an attractive quiche, accompanied by wholewheat bread and a tossed green salad.

FILLING
*2 medium avocados*
*125 g cheddar cheese, grated*
*1 onion, finely chopped*
*2 eggs, beaten*
*50 ml milk*
*Salt & black pepper to taste*

PASTRY
*200 g cake flour*
*Pinch salt*
*50 g butter, chilled*
*50 g lard, chilled*
*30 ml (2T) cold water*

Prepare the pastry ahead: Sift the flour and salt into a bowl, rub in the butter and lard lightly with your fingertips. Use a knife to mix the cold water in lightly but well. Cover dough and chill in refrigerator for 30 minutes. Roll out and use to line a quiche dish.

FOR THE FILLING: Dice the avocados, which should be ripe. Mix the grated cheese and onion with the eggs and milk. Add the diced avocado and season to taste. Spoon the mixture over the pastry-lined dish. Bake at 180 °C for 30–45 minutes, or until set and golden brown. (The avocado will retain its fresh colour in this quiche.) Serve hot or cold, with salad.

*Natal*

# Sweetcorn Muffins

Makes 12
Excellent, nutritious muffins for a picnic lunch – they do not need to be served warm.

*1 × 420 g can sweetcorn (cream style)*
*500 ml (2 cups) brown bread flour*
*15 ml (3t) baking powder*
*2 ml (1/2t) salt*
*2 eggs, lightly beaten*
*125 ml plain yogurt or buttermilk*
*60 ml (4T) melted butter*

Sift the flour, baking powder and salt into a bowl. Mix the beaten eggs with the yogurt/buttermilk and melted butter, then pour into a well in the dry ingredients. Mix thoroughly. Add the sweetcorn and mix well.

Spoon the mixture into greased muffin tins, filling them three-quarters of the way. (The batter makes 12 large muffins). Bake for 20–25 minutes at 200 °C. Leave to cool in the muffin tin for a few minutes before removing. To serve, split and butter.

*Western Cape*

# Mealiemeal Muffins

Makes 12
A great way to serve the traditional maize- or mealiemeal accompaniment to Transvaal braais – not "pap" but delightful muffins baked in the oven.

*250 ml (1 cup) maize meal/mealiemeal*
*250 ml (1 cup) flour*
*Pinch salt*
*20 ml (4t) baking powder*
*30 ml (2T) sugar*
*1 egg*
*250 ml (1 cup) milk*
*45 ml (3T) melted butter or margarine*

Sift the maize meal, flour, salt and baking powder together; add the sugar. Beat the egg, adding the milk and melted butter; pour into a well in the dry ingredients and mix quickly and well.

Grease muffin pans and fill three-quarters full with the batter. Bake in oven preheated to 200 °C for about 25 minutes (watch them at the end to avoid burning). Split while warm and butter at once; serve warm with the braai or with a winter supper of soup.

*Transvaal*

# Maize Bread for the Braai

Serves 8–10
An outstanding accompaniment for the braai – delicious maize (mealie) bread, traditional in the Transvaal.

*375 ml (1½ cups) milk*
*375 ml (1½ cups) maize meal (mieliemeal)*
*60 ml (4T) butter*
*3 eggs, beaten*
*250 ml (1 cup) flour*
*15 ml (1T) baking powder*
*30 ml (2T) sugar*
*5 ml (1t) salt*
*5 ml (1t) dried sage*
*250 ml (1 cup) chopped celery*
*180 ml (3/4 cup) grated carrot*
*1 large onion, chopped*
*1 small green pepper, chopped*

Bring the milk to the boil and pour over the maize meal in a bowl. Add the butter, stir well and allow to cool thoroughly. Mix the beaten eggs into the maize meal mixture, then add all the remaining ingredients and mix in well.

Place mixture in a flat greased ovenware dish and bake in an oven preheated to 200 °C for about 40 minutes, or until baked through. Cut into squares and serve warm with the grilled meat.

*Transvaal*

# Fantan Rolls

Makes about 36 rolls
Children especially love these rolls for the braai, because they can peel off layers and eat them one by delicious one – with or without butter.

*7 cups flour*
*1 packet instant dried yeast (10g)*
*5 ml (1t) salt*
*125 ml (1/2 cup) sugar (or less to taste)*
*2 eggs, beaten*
*125 ml (1/2 cup) cooking oil*
*500 ml (2 cups) lukewarm water*

Sift the dry ingredients together. Beat the eggs and the oil together, then add to the lukewarm water in a bowl. Now sift the dry ingredients a second time, into the liquids. Stir until the dough begins to hold together. Knead very well for 10–15 minutes. Oil a bowl and roll the dough in the oil to coat it. Cover the dough-bowl with plastic wrap and leave to stand in a warm place until dough has doubled in size. (This will depend on the degree of warmth and the weather – it could take several hours.)

Punch down the dough, and cut into 4 portions. Roll each one separately into a rectangle (about 30 mm thick). Brush with oil and cut into strips 5 cm wide. Layer these strips one on top of the other (see diagram). With a sharp knife, cut into squares 5 cm wide. Turn the squares cut side up and place in well greased muffin tins. Allow to rise until doubled in size.

Bake in oven preheated to 180 °C for 15 minutes, or until well browned.

*Transvaal*

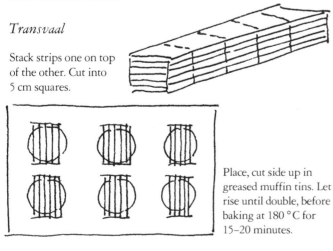

Stack strips one on top of the other. Cut into 5 cm squares.

Place, cut side up in greased muffin tins. Let rise until double, before baking at 180 °C for 15–20 minutes.

# Bread Rolls with Chicken Liver Stuffing

Serves 6
Delicious and easy dish for an alfresco family meal. Use crusty rolls with poppy or sesame seeds on top.

*6 fresh round rolls*
*500 g chicken livers, cut into chunks*
*300 g mushrooms, chopped*
*Oil and butter (or margarine) for frying*
*1 small onion, chopped finely*
*125 ml (1/2 cup) brandy*
*125 ml (1/2 cup) white wine*
*125 ml (1/2 cup) chicken stock*
*250 ml (1 cup) fresh cream*
*(OR 250 ml (1 cup) yoghurt stabilised by adding 10 ml (2t) cornflour)*
*15 ml (1T) fresh thyme, chopped*
*(OR 5 ml (1t) dried thyme)*
*45 ml (3T) French or whole-grain mustard*
*60 ml (1/4 cup) parsley, finely chopped*

Remove the tops of the rolls and hollow them out carefully, keeping the crumbs for another use (or see tip below). Fry the livers and mushrooms in the oil/butter mixture until nearly done. Put them aside and pour any extra fat out of the pan. Add the chopped onion, brandy, wine and stock to the still-hot pan, put back on high heat and reduce the liquid by half. Then add all remaining ingredients except the parsley to the pan and simmer for 3 minutes. (At this stage, if the mixture is too liquid, crumble in some of the breadcrumbs you saved; however, if the liquid is reduced properly, this shouldn't be necessary.)

Spoon the mixture into the hollowed rolls, sprinkle with parsley and replace tops of rolls. (NOTE: Do not keep these rolls hot for a long time, as the filling might soften the bottom of the rolls too much.) Serve with a tossed green salad and wine.

*Transvaal*

## Baked Mealies & Tomato

Serves 6

A good side dish for a braai, or with cold meats or fish mayonnaise at lunch. It is best to strip fresh, uncooked mealies (corn) from the cob, but canned kernels would be a short cut. However, the tomatoes are best fresh, since canned tomatoes tend to have an overpowering taste.

*500 ml (2 cups) green mealie/corn kernels*
*200 g fresh tomatoes, peeled & chopped*
*5 ml (1t) sugar*
*Salt & freshly ground black pepper to taste*
*1 egg, beaten*
*250 ml (1 cup) fresh breadcrumbs*
*Butter*

Note: If you use canned mealies and they are the sweet-corn variety, omit the sugar in the following.

Mix the mealie kernels and tomato pulp with the sugar, salt & pepper to taste, and finally the beaten egg. Pour into a greased baking dish and sprinkle the breadcrumbs over. Dot with butter and bake in a moderate oven (180 °C) for 25–30 minutes or until golden brown on top.

*Transvaal*

## Margie's Pumpkin

Serves 8

An unusual whole baked pumpkin dish – and a good talking point – to serve on the side for outdoor eating.

*1 medium pumpkin*
*2 large onions, chopped finely*
*Butter*
*300 ml fresh breadcrumbs*
*250 ml (1 cup) Emmenthal cheese, grated*
*2 ml (1/2t) freshly grated nutmeg*
*Salt & black pepper to taste*
*250 ml (1 cup) cream*

Cut a neat lid in the top of the pumpkin; remove the seeds carefully and scrape clean inside. Sauté the onion in butter until soft but not browned. Stir in the breadcrumbs and cheese, adding the nutmeg and seasoning to taste. Fill the pumpkin with the mixture, closing its lid. Place the pumpkin in a large dish, pouring hot water in round the sides to come three-quarter way up the dish. Bake in oven preheated to 180 °C for 2½ hours; keep topping up the hot water. When the pumpkin is cooked, remove from the oven and carefully stir in the cream. Serve immediately.

*Eastern Cape*

## Picnic Fillet of Beef

Serves 6

Few countries use whole fillets of beef the way South Africans do – but for an alfresco meal there are few things to beat the sight of the pink, succulent slices, and there's no fat or wastage to detract from the treat.

*1,5 kg fillet of beef*
*2 large cloves garlic*
*45 ml (3T) soy sauce*
*60 g butter*

Trim and tie the fillet securely. Crush the garlic and spread over the meat. Pour over the soy sauce and leave to marinate for an hour or more, turning occasionally.

Preheat oven to 220 °C. Meanwhile, on top of the stove, sear the fillet by heating the butter in a heavy-bottomed iron casserole and turning the fillet in the sizzling butter to seal on all sides. Put straight into the oven for 20–25 minutes, turning once and basting. Remove from the oven and cool in the juices, turning occasionally.

Slice thinly and serve with creamed horseradish, crisp rolls and green salad.

*Orange Free State*

# Beef Fillet-in-a-Loaf

Serves 6–8

A very different way to do a whole fillet over the coals – it is equally nice the next day, served cold in slices, with salads. Do use a good pâté, or a really tasty liver spread if you must, for the best flavour.

*1 × 1,5 kg beef fillet*
*1 loaf milk bread*
*Freshly ground black pepper*
*60 ml (4T) butter or margarine*
*60 ml (1/4 cup) brandy*
*125 g mushrooms, chopped*
*2 rashers bacon, rind removed & chopped*
*250 g liver pâté*
*30ml (2T) red wine*
*Fresh parsley, chopped*

You will need a loaf of milk bread and a whole fillet of beef for this interesting dish. Trim beef and rub with pepper. Tie the fillet to retain its shape. Heat the butter in a frying pan, add the meat and sear on all sides over a good heat. Pour over the brandy, warm and ignite. Cover the pan and cook beef very gently in the brandy for 10 minutes, using a low heat and turning the fillet frequently. (This works well in a waterless pot.) Remove fillet and set aside.

Add chopped mushrooms and bacon to the pan, cook gently, then stir in the liver pâté and wine.

Cut a slice lengthwise off the top of the bread and scoop out the inside, leaving about a 2,5 cm crust. Spread a layer of the bacon, mushroom and liver pâté mixture over the inner surface of the loaf, including the "lid" Remove string from fillet and place in the loaf. Sprinkle with the parsley and cover with the top crust. Place on a greased sheet of aluminium foil and roll up tightly. Place on moderately hot coals and cook for about 30 minutes, turning frequently.

Remove, cut the fillet-in-a-loaf into slices (this is best done with an electric carving knife) and serve with a green salad. The fillet should still be beautifully pink in the middle, and the bread will have absorbed some of the wonderful juices along with the pâté mixture.

*Transvaal*

# Vegetable Potjiekos

Serves 6

An excellent vegetarian potjie dish (you could use practically any choice of vegetables with this method, barring beetroot and spinach) – or you can add a middle layer of seasoned chicken or beef (such as shin), or flaked smoked snoek – but then be careful with the salt!

INGREDIENTS
*3 large onions, sliced*
*1 large aubergine/brinjal, unpeeled & cubed*
*3 red or green peppers, sliced in strips*
*250 ml (1 cup) green beans, cut in half*
*3 courgettes/baby marrows, sliced*
*250 ml (1 cup) celery, chopped*
*2 potatoes, sliced thinly*
*250 ml (1 cup) cabbage, shredded*
*250 ml (1 cup) carrots, sliced*
*2 green mealies, cut from the cob*
*1 small cauliflower, cut into florets*

*3 medium tomatoes, skinned & chopped*
*250 ml (1 cup) seedless grapes*
*250 ml (1 cup) frozen peas*

SAUCE
*250 ml (1 cup) sunflower oil*
*4 cloves garlic, crushed*
*45 ml (3T) fresh parsley, chopped*
*2 bayleaves, crumbled*
*10 ml (2t) dried thyme*
*10 ml (2t) dried marjoram*
*25 ml (5t) salt*
*2 ml (1/2t) chilli powder, or to taste*

Prepare vegetables. Beat the ingredients for the sauce together. Lightly oil the potjie and layer the vegetables, sprinkling each layer with the sauce – use the vegetables in the order listed, ending with the cauliflower. Cover tightly and cook gently for 90 minutes, or longer if meat or chicken have been added.

Finally place the tomatoes, grapes and peas on top of the potjiekos, sprinkle with the last of the sauce and cover again; cook for 15 minutes longer. Serve hot with brown rice, or use to stuff pockets of pita bread.

*Transvaal*

# Mixed Kebabs for the Braai

Serves 12
From marinated ingredients, guests assemble their own kebabs to cook over the coals.

*600 g pork fillet*
*600 g deboned leg of lamb*
*500 g chicken breast fillets*
*500 g smoked sausage*
*600 g boerewors*
*500 g bacon*
*250 g button mushrooms*
*500 g baby onions, peeled*
*2 green peppers*
*1 pineapple*
*250 g dried fruit, soaked until soft*

MARINADE
*100 ml soy sauce*
*100 ml honey*
*50 ml tomato sauce*
*50 ml vinegar*
*30 ml (2T) sherry*
*30 ml (2T) water*
*10 ml (2t) brown sugar*
*10 ml (2t) chicken stock powder*
*2 cloves garlic, crushed*

Cube the pork, lamb and chicken breasts. Slice the sausages. Mix the marinade ingredients together and marinate the meat for a few hours or ovenight. Cut the bacon, vegetables and fruit into suitable chunks for the skewers. Place each ingredient in a separate bowl and have plenty of wooden skewers ready for the guests to assemble their own kebabs.

Have a good fire, salads, crusty bread and a couple of tasty sauces such as the following:

CURRIED MAYONNAISE: Mix 125 ml (1/2 cup) mayonnaise, 125 ml (1/2 cup) apricot jam, and 15 ml (1T) curry powder mixed with a little water.

MUSTARD SAUCE: Mix 125 ml (1/2 cup) vinegar, 125 ml (1/2 cup) water, 125 ml (1/2 cup) sugar (this is optional) and 15 ml (1T) mustard powder in a saucepan. Add 2 eggs and heat, whisking continuously, to just below boiling point. Add 10 ml (2t) cornflour mixed with a little water; bring the sauce to just below boiling point again, then remove from heat and leave to cool before serving.

*Natal*

# Venison Kebabs

Makes 12 kebabs
Choice fillet of rooibok – impala – is used for these marinated treats for the braai (springbok would be an alternative). Pawpaw in the marinade is an excellent natural tenderising agent.

*2 kg rooibok fillet, cubed*
*12 dried fruit patties (mebos), cubed*
*Black mushrooms, quartered*
*24 rashers streaky bacon, rolled & sliced*
*1 large green pepper, cubed*

MARINADE
*300 ml dry white wine*
*125 ml (1/2 cup) honey*
*125 ml (1/2 cup) tomato puree*
*15 ml (1T) Worcestershire sauce*
*150 g pawpaw pulp*
*5 ml (1t) curry powder*
*15 ml (1T) mixed fresh herbs, chopped*
*100 ml sunflower oil*

The cubed venison is to be marinated for 3 days. For the marinade, bring the wine, honey, tomato puree and Worcestershire sauce to the boil in a saucepan. Cool before adding the pawpaw pulp, flavourings and oil. Pour over the venison cubes and stir well; store in the refrigerator for 3 days, stirring occasionally. When the kebabs are to be assembled, drain the venison, reserving some of the marinade as a basting sauce.

Thread onto skewers the cubed venison, dried fruit (mebos), mushroom pieces, bacon rolls and green pepper. Cook over medium hot coals, brushing with the marinade, until done. Serve with pap (maize meal porridge), tomato gravy and fresh salads.

*Natal*

## Stuffed Flat-Chicken Potjie

(Illustrated on page 48)

Serves 6
Butterflied chicken, plumped up beautifully with a stuffing under the skin, is cooked to a turn in a potjie.

*1 × 1,5 kg fresh chicken*
*Salt & freshly ground black pepper*
*1 large garlic clove, crushed*
*5 ml (1t) dried marjoram & paprika mixed*
*15 ml (1T) lemon juice*

STUFFING
*500 g cooked rice*
*250 g fresh breadcrumbs*
*1 onion, finely chopped*
*2 strips bacon, chopped*
*Half a green pepper, chopped*
*1 large clove garlic, crushed*
*10 ml (2t) salt*
*Freshly ground black pepper to taste*
*Fresh parsley, chopped*
*Fresh rosemary & origanum, chopped*
*15 ml (1T) lemon juice*

BASTING SAUCE
*2 chicken cubes*
*500 ml (2 cups) hot water*
*250 ml (1 cup) dry white wine*
*2 bayleaves*

*30 ml (2T) apricot jam*
*30 ml (2T) cooking oil*
*6 medium potatoes*

Cut the chicken down the breast and "butterfly" it to flatten it. Then loosen the skin carefully, starting from the tail and around the thighs. Rub into the skin the salt and pepper, garlic, marjoram and paprika, and sprinkle the lemon juice over.

Mix the stuffing ingredients (because rice can be bland, don't forget the pepper!) and stuff the chicken between the flesh and skin, and into the thighs. Flatten the stuffing by patting the chicken's back; secure skin with toothpicks to prevent mixture falling out.

Have ready the basting sauce, dissolving the chicken cubes in the water and adding the wine and bayleaves. Rub 15 ml (1T) of the apricot jam onto the chicken.

Heat the cooking oil in a flat-bottomed cast iron pot and place the chicken on its back; turn it in the hot oil for 2–4 minutes until the skin is golden brown. Now turn the chicken into a butterfly position in the pot and pour in about half of the basting sauce. Cover and decrease heat of fire or place pot over slower coals – it must cook slowly for about 1½ hours. Add sauce as needed. For the last 45 minutes or so, peel the potatoes, roll in the rest of the apricot jam and place round the chicken in the pot; cover and complete cooking. Serve hot with salads, crusty bread and wine.

*Western Cape*

## Oxtail Potjiekos

Serves 6–8
Slow cooking develops the full oxtail savour.

*2 oxtails*
*Seasoned flour*
*5 ml (1t) dried thyme*
*80 ml (1/3 cup) cooking oil*
*1 clove garlic, crushed*
*500 ml (2 cups) water*
*250 ml (1 cup) dry red wine*
*4 potatoes, cubed*
*3 carrots, sliced*
*12 baby onions, peeled*
*125 g button mushrooms*
*2 sticks celery, chopped*
*1 × 115 g can tomato paste*
*Salt & black pepper to taste*

Joint oxtails, wipe and toss in seasoned flour and thyme. Heat the oil in a large frying pan and brown oxtail pieces well. Remove with slotted spoon and place in cast-iron potjie. Pour off excess fat from pan, add garlic, water and wine and bring to the boil, stirring. Add to the oxtail in the potjie. Cook, covered, over the coals for 3 hours. Add vegetables and tomato paste. Season, cover again and return to the fire. Cook for 1 hour more. Skim off any excess fat before serving with rice and salad.

*Transvaal*

63

# Venison Potjie Roast

Serves 8–10

You may cook this as an ordinary pot roast, but somehow it is more tasty done over the fire. The dish has been made with springbok, duiker, bushbuck, rhebuck and even fallow deer. Great for camping, when only buttered bread is needed besides.

*1,5 kg leg of venison*
*10 ml (2t) butter*
*2 medium onions, sliced*
*4 large potatoes*
*10 ml (2t) cooking oil*
*Salt & pepper to taste*
*2 rashers bacon*
*4 leaves spinach*
*4 medium carrots*
*2 medium tomatoes*
*3 sprigs parsley*
*Pinch dried mixed herbs*
*Pinch ground allspice*
*1 × 420 g can mixed vegetables (or use frozen)*

Warm pot over low heat, add butter and when melted add the sliced onion and one of the potatoes, sliced. Brown, then add the cooking oil. Now, over a hotter flame, brown the venison, searing both sides. Add water to cover the meat three-quarters of the way. Add all the other ingredients except the tinned vegetables and remaining potatoes.

Cover the pot and bring to the boil. Add salt and pepper to taste and then allow to simmer over a low flame for about 8 hours. Add the other 3 potatoes, sliced, and simmer again for 30 minutes or until potatoes are cooked. Add the mixed vegetables and heat through before serving. The liquid should have cooked down to form a delicious gravy which shouldn't need thickening. Serve with rice and a salad.

*Eastern Cape*

# Wildevy Venison Potjiekos

Serves 8

Venison – impala, wildebeest and warthog are suggestions – is marinated in a surprising way and cooked for long hours in a three-legged or flat-bottomed potjie.

*1 leg of venison*
*2 litres Coca Cola*
*30 ml (2T) cooking oil*
*5 onions, sliced*
*500 g dried apricots or peaches*
*(OR 6 Granny Smith apples, chopped)*
*500 g dried prunes*
*6 cloves garlic, finely chopped*
*2 ml (1/2t) ground cloves*
*5 ml (1t) dried thyme*
*Salt & black pepper to taste*
*Butter*

Marinate the leg for 24 hours in the cooldrink; wipe dry, reserving the marinade. Heat the oil in the potjie and brown the meat well. Add the onions and brown them, then add all the other ingredients except the butter. Add a little of the marinade to keep the mixture moist. Cover and cook at a low heat over coals for 4–5 hours, adding marinade from time to time to make a fairly thick gravy.

Before serving, add a large knob of butter. The venison will be tender and not in the least dry. It is excellent served with pumpkin and Pommes Anna, both done in cast-iron pots, and a green vegetable.

*Transvaal*

*Opposite:* Golden Chicken with Honey Mustard Sauce has the winning flavour. *Prepared with choice ingredients from Woolworths Overleaf: (left)* South African beef casserole; and *(right)* Karoo Lamb with Olives – *both photographed with wines from Woolwoths' special range and prepared with Woolworths ingredients Page 68:* Ostrich Fillet Sosaties, succulent cubes cooked in the pan

# Meat, Game & Chicken

# Meat, Game & Chicken

*Chicken Dishes*
Bacon & Chicken Liver Lasagne, 74
Chicken Pieces in Batter, 72
Chicken with Apricots, 71
Golden Chicken with Honey Mustard Sauce, 71
Lemon Chicken Plait, 73
Sunshine Chicken, 72
Tipsy Tropical Chicken, 74

*Lamb Dishes*
Karoo Lamb with Olives, 75
Kerrieboontjiesbredie (Bredie of Curried Beans), 75
Lamb Curry, 76
Sweet & Sour Lamb's Tongues, 76

*Beef & Veal Dishes*
Boer Bobotie Pie, 79
Braised Beef with Anchovies, 79
Casseroled Steak with Sweet Potatoes, 77
Frikkadels with Sour Cream Sauce, 77
Kofta Curry, 78
Marinated Veal Cutlets, 81
South African Beef Casserole, 78

*Pork Dishes*
Baked Kassler Rib with Red Cabbage, 80
Pork & Plums, 80

*Venison & Game Birds*
Marinating Venison, 85

Guinea Fowl Jubilee, 84
Guinea Fowl Stew, 84
Jugged Venison, Hare or Guinea Fowl, 83
Ostrich Fillet Sosaties in the Pan, 83
Roast Leg of Venison, 86
Roast Leg of Wild Pig, 82
Saddle of Venison, 85
Sweet-Sour Rabbit, 82
Venison Bobotie, 81

## Golden Chicken with Honey Mustard Sauce

(Illustrated on page 65)

Serves 5–6
Chicken pieces with a truly magnificent flavour and appearance, coated in a pale gold sauce.

*10 chicken thighs*
*60 g butter*
*5 ml (1t) seasoned salt*
*1 chicken cube, crumbled*
*5 ml (1t) curry powder*
*50 ml wholegrain French mustard*
*75 ml honey*
*5 ml (1t) lemon juice*
*125 ml (1/2 cup) cream*
*Orange slices & fresh herbs for garnish*

Use chicken thighs for the best result with this dish. Melt the butter, add the salt, stock powder, curry powder, mustard and honey, and roll the chicken pieces in this mixture. Place in an ovenproof casserole dish in which the pieces fit closely together but do not overlap. Pour over any remaining sauce, cover with foil and leave to marinate for 5–6 hours for the flavour to develop.

Preheat oven to 180 °C. Bake chicken, still covered, in the marinade for 1 hour. Remove from oven and strain all the juice into a saucepan. Replace chicken in oven uncovered, and bake for a further 15–20 minutes until chicken is tender and a lovely deep gold (be careful not to burn the dish at this stage).

Keep chicken pieces warm while you make the sauce: Skim off any fat from the juices in the saucepan, and reduce by boiling briskly, adding the lemon juice. Keep tasting until the flavour is strong and good, then add the cream and continue reducing the sauce – but over low heat now, so as not to allow the cream to boil. You should find you have a thick, pale gold sauce with a magnificently full flavour.

Place the chicken pieces on a serving platter and pour the sauce over (or serve separately). Garnish platter with orange slices and fresh herbs or watercress. This dish goes especially well with wheatrice or brown rice tossed with mushrooms and spring onions, and a good green salad.

*Western Cape*

## Chicken with Apricots

Serves 6
Chicken casserole with a sweet apricot sauce is a firm favourite in South Africa.

*12 chicken pieces*
*15 ml (1T) olive or sunflower oil*
*Salt & black pepper to taste*
*5 ml (1t) ground ginger*
*Lemon juice*
*1 × 825 g can apricots*
*Juice & rind of 1 orange*
*125 ml (1/2 cup) golden syrup (optional)*
*5 ml (1t) ground ginger*
*5 ml (1t) soya sauce*
*5 ml (1t) lemon juice*

Rub the chicken pieces with the oil and season well with the salt, pepper and ground ginger. Sprinkle with a little lemon juice and cook under the hot grill until the chicken is well browned. This should take about 10 minutes. Remove chicken to a large ovenproof casserole with a lid.

Puree the apricots and their juice in a blender (dieters would prefer to use a can with no extra sugar added). Pour into a saucepan and add the juice and rind of the orange, the syrup (optional), the ground ginger, soya sauce and lemon juice. Bring to the boil and pour over the chicken pieces in the casserole. Cover and place in oven preheated to 180 °C for 20 minutes. Remove lid and bake for a further 10 minutes, checking that the chicken is fully cooked.

Serve hot with rice and salad – but this dish is also good cold with salads.

*Eastern Cape*

## Chicken Pieces in Batter

Serves 6
Fried chicken pieces in batter have become another South African favourite, though the method hails from the Deep South of the United States. This is not for the calorie-conscious; serve with a healthy green salad to compensate!

*1 large chicken, skinned & cut into pieces*
*(OR 12 bought chicken pieces, skinned)*

MARINADE
*80 ml (1/3 cup) soya sauce*
*80 ml (1/3 cup) dry white wine*
*Pinch breyani masala (or mild curry powder)*
*Pinch ground ginger*
*2 ml (1/2t) paprika*
*5 ml (1t) dried rosemary*
*Freshly ground white or black pepper*
*2 cloves garlic, crushed (or to taste)*

BATTER
*500 ml (2 cups) selfraising flour*
*2 ml (1/2t) salt*
*2 egg yolks (reserve whites)*
*15 ml (1T) cooking oil*
*80 ml (1/3 cup) water*
*250 ml (1 cup) flat beer (or water)*

*2 egg whites, whisked with pinch salt*
*Cooking oil for deep frying*
*Fresh watercress & lemon twists for garnish*

Cut the chicken into serving pieces (eg 4 pieces breast, 4 of leg/thigh, 2 wings); keep unused bits for the stockpot.

MARINADE: Mix all the ingredients well together in a deep container and marinate the chicken pieces for 8 hours, or overnight, keeping them in the refrigerator. Turn the pieces occasionally.

About 2 hours before the dish is needed, prepare the BATTER: Sift the flour and salt, mix the egg yolks with the oil and 80 ml water, and then add to the flour; add sufficient of the flat beer (or extra water) to make a batter with a soft, dropping consistency. Cover the bowl and store in the refrigerator to chill.

(Keep the egg whites at room temperature until needed.)

Put the chicken pieces in a saucepan with the marinade and an additional 500 ml (2 cups) water, heat and simmer for about 15 minutes until virtually cooked. (Alternately, pressure cook for 5 minutes.) When the chicken pieces are cool enough to handle, dry with a paper towel and flour them lightly.

Heat cooking oil in a deep fryer to 180 °C (or until it takes 1 minute for a cube of bread to turn brown). Meanwhile whisk the egg whites with the salt until just beginning to form peaks. Mix a small portion of this into the batter to make it airy, then fold the rest in gently.

Dip floured chicken one piece at a time in the batter, covering it completely, then immerse in the hot oil and fry. Do not crowd the fryer. Turn pieces and cook until golden. Drain on absorbent paper and keep warm till all are done.

Serve in a napkin-lined basket, or on a platter, decorated with fresh watercress and twists of lemon.

*Transvaal*

## Sunshine Chicken

Serves 6
Chicken breast fillets are an increasingly popular choice – here is another tasty way to use them, with asparagus tips.

*6 chicken breast fillets*
*Salt & black pepper*
*Flour to coat chicken*
*2 eggs, lightly beaten*
*250 g breadcrumbs*
*250 g butter*
*75 ml brown stock*
*75 ml white wine*
*50 g mushrooms, sliced*
*20 ml (4t) lemon juice*
*2 × 290 g cans asparagus tips, drained*

Season the chicken breast fillets well with salt and black pepper, freshly ground. Coat with flour, dip in the egg, then roll in the breadcrumbs to coat the pieces well. Chill for 30 minutes to firm the fillets. Heat about 150 g of the butter in a large frying pan and sauté the crumbed breasts until cooked through and golden outside. Drain and keep warm on a serving platter. To the same frying pan add the stock and wine, incorporating the tasty scrapings in the pan; simmer for 3 minutes or so, then add the mushrooms. Bring back to the boil, stir in about 40 g of the butter and add the lemon juice. Check for seasoning. Pour the hot sauce over the chicken pieces and keep warm.

Melt the remaining butter in a saucepan and heat the asparagus tips, shaking well to coat them with butter without breaking them. Arrange round the chicken and serve at once with rice and a green salad.

*Transvaal*

# Lemon Chicken Plait

Serves 4–6
A rich and satisfying chicken dish with a lovely lemony flavour.

*4 chicken breast fillets, skinned*
*50 g butter or margarine*
*50 g button mushrooms, quartered*
*50 g flour*
*250 ml (1 cup) milk*
*1 chicken stock cube*
*Rind & juice of half a lemon*
*15 ml (1T) fresh parsley, chopped*
*Salt & freshly ground pepper to taste*

PASTRY
*250 g flour*
*2 ml (1/2t) salt*
*60 g margarine, diced*
*60 g butter, diced*
*100 ml cold water to mix*
*Beaten egg to brush over*

*Garnish of lemon slices & fresh parsley*

Dice the chicken breasts. Heat the butter or margarine in a saucepan and fry the chicken and mushrooms until browned. Stir in the flour, cook a minute longer, then remove from the heat and add milk and crumble in the stock cube. Return to the heat, bring to the boil stirring continuously, and cook until the sauce thickens. Add the lemon rind and juice and the parsley, cooking for one or two minutes. Test for seasoning, and leave to cool.

TO MAKE PASTRY: Preheat oven to 200 °C. Sift flour and salt into bowl and rub in shortening until mixture resembles fine breadcrumbs. Add the cold water and mix to form a firm dough. Turn out onto floured board and knead lightly; leave to rest for 30 minutes. Roll out pastry and trim to 30 cm square. Place on greased baking tray. Spread chicken filling in 10 cm panel down middle of the pastry. On either side of the filling, cut pastry into 15 mm strips. Brush the edges of these with beaten egg and fold across the filling, working alternately from either side to create a plaited effect. Brush with beaten egg and bake for 30 minutes or until golden. Cool on wire rack.

Place chicken plait on serving platter and garnish with lemon slices and parsley. Serve with a tossed green salad.

*Natal*

# Tipsy Tropical Chicken

Serves 6–8

An interesting combination of tastes, textures and colours in a chicken dish ideal for entertaining – you can make it ahead, as the taste is enhanced by keeping the dish overnight. Do not omit the stuffed olives, which provide an essential flavour.

*1,5 kg chicken, cut into serving pieces*
*500 ml (2 cups) dry white wine*
*Flour seasoned with salt & pepper*
*Oil or butter to fry chicken pieces*
*1 large onion, chopped*
*4 large tomatoes, peeled & chopped*
*(OR 1 × 400 g can peeled tomatoes, drained & chopped)*
*5 ml (1t) dried thyme*
*5 ml (1t) sweet basil, chopped*
*Good pinch cayenne*
*(OR good dash Tabasco or chilli sauce)*
*3 carrots, scraped & chopped*
*3 potatoes, peeled & cut into chunks*
*250 ml stuffed green olives*
*12 prunes*
*4 bananas, sliced thickly*
*45 ml (3T) sugar*
*2–4 cloves garlic, chopped or crushed*
*Salt & pepper to taste*

Marinate the chicken pices overnight in the wine; drain, reserving the wine. Roll the chicken pieces in the seasoned flour, heat the oil in a frying pan and brown the chicken on both sides. Add the onion, tomato (squeeze out any excess juice first) and reserved wine. Cover and simmer gently for 30 minutes.

Add the herbs, cayenne or Tabasco, carrots and potatoes. Simmer gently for another 45 minutes. (At this stage, the dish may be cooled and kept in the refrigerator overnight.) Now add the olives, prunes (removing the stones first), banana and sugar. Stir with care – the vegetables and fruit should not be broken up. Cook for 10–15 minutes over gentle heat. Finally add the garlic, stirring in gently, and test for seasoning. Serve with yellow rice and sliced avocado.

*Transvaal*

# Bacon & Chicken Liver Lasagne

Serves 6

For those who are tired of the usual style of lasagne, a supper dish with a difference.

*125 g rindless bacon, finely chopped*
*500 g chicken livers*
*500 g ribbon noodles*
*2 medium onions, chopped*
*30 ml (2T) oil or butter*
*1 × 290 g can asparagus pieces*
*1 × 400 g can peeled tomatoes*
*125 g mushrooms, sliced*
*White sauce made with 750 ml milk plus asparagus juice and 250 ml (1 cup) grated cheddar cheese*

Cook the noodles in plenty of boiling salted water, drain and rinse with cold water; set aside. Sauté the onions in the oil till transparant, add the bacon and chicken livers and fry another 5 minutes or so. Drain the asparagus pieces (reserving the juice for the white sauce), and add the asparagus to the pan. Drain and chop the peeled tomatoes (save the juice for some other purpose) and add together with the mushrooms. Season with freshly ground black pepper to taste.

Prepare the white sauce, and add grated cheddar cheese seasoning it with salt and pepper to taste. To layer the lasagne, use a large rectangular ovenproof dish and place a layer of noodles on the base, then the chicken liver/bacon mix, and repeat this until ingredients are used up. Now pour over all the cheese sauce, and check for seasoning. Sprinkle top with extra grated cheese. Bake in oven preheated to 180 °C for 20 minutes or until top is bubbly and golden. Serve with a green salad and a crisp white wine.

*Western Cape*

# Karoo Lamb with Olives

(Illustrated on page 67)

Serves 6–8

An outstanding Mediterranean flavour from a dish based on our famous, succulent Karoo lamb. Don't be alarmed at the large amount of garlic – it is perfectly delicious, and no one need fear smelling of garlic when the cloves are cooked whole in this way! For a more economical dish, you may use good stewing lamb.

*1,5 –2 kg leg of lamb, cubed*
*250 ml (1 cup) black olives, pitted & halved*
*250 ml (1 cup) garlic cloves, peeled & left whole*
*1 × 410 g can tomato puree*
*60 ml (1/4 cup) red wine (optional)*
*1 large onion, chopped*
*250 ml (1 cup) fresh parsley, chopped*
*125 ml (1/2 cup) celery leaves, chopped*
*5 ml (1t) dried basil or 15 ml (1T) fresh basil, chopped*
*2 ml (1/2t) dried origanum or 5 ml (1t) fresh origanum, chopped*
*10 ml (2t) salt*
*2 ml (1/2t) sugar*
*2 ml (1/2t) freshly ground black pepper*

Have the butcher debone and cube the lamb, trimming it of excess fat. Mix all the ingredients together in a heavy casserole dish with a tight-fitting lid, reserving a third of the parsley for garnishing. (To ensure no steam escapes from the casserole, you may cover with foil under the lid.) Preheat the oven to 180 °C and cook the lamb for about 1 hour. Take out to stir, then reduce heat to 150 °C and cook for a further 50–60 minutes, or until the meat is tender. Garnish with remaining parsley and serve with rice and a fresh green vegetable such as broccoli.

*Natal*

# Kerrieboontjiesbredie (Bredie of Curried Beans)

Serves 6

A gently spiced bredie of lamb and haricot beans that improves with long cooking. You could use tinned butter beans as a short cut, but give the flavours time to develop.

*750 g boneless shoulder of lamb*
*500 g small haricot beans*
*3 medium onions, chopped*
*2 large cloves garlic, chopped or crushed*
*2 pinches chilli powder*
*60 ml (4T) sunflower oil*
*Salt & freshly ground black pepper to taste*
*10 ml (2t) masala/curry powder (or more to taste)*
*30 ml (2T) lemon juice*
*2ml (1/2t) brown sugar*

Ask the butcher to slice the lamb thinly. Soak the dried beans overnight in cold water, drain, cover with fresh water and bring to the boil in a large saucepan. Cook gently, covered, for 30 minutes or until the beans are almost cooked – they should still be nutty to the bite. Drain, reserving the cooking liquid.

Sprinkle the chopped onions with the chilli powder and add the garlic. In a heavy-bottomed casserole/saucepan, heat the sunflower oil and stir in the onion/garlic mix, and sauté until golden. Lay the sliced meat on the onion and remove from the heat. Sprinkle salt and pepper over to taste. Mix the curry powder with the lemon juice and sugar, and pour over the meat. Cover and simmer for 10 minutes.

Now add the cooked beans and enough of their liquid to provide a good gravy (about 300 ml). Sprinkle extra salt and black pepper over the beans, to taste. Cover and cook over low heat or in a slow oven (140 °C) until the meat and beans are very tender – the longer the better, as this improves the flavour. Check seasoning before serving with crusty bread to mop up the juices, and a green salad to follow.

*Natal*

## Sweet & Sour Lamb's Tongues

Serves 6
An unusual and quite delectable dish for a supper or luncheon.

*8–10 lamb's tongues*
*1 clove of garlic, crushed*
*1 onion, chopped*
*1 bayleaf, crushed*
*125 ml (1/2 cup) seedless raisins*
*30 ml (2T) brown sugar*
*5 ml (1t) salt*
*30 ml (2T) wholewheat flour, mixed with 60 ml (1/4 cup) water*
*Freshly ground black pepper*
*15–30 ml (1–2T) vinegar or lemon juice*

Steam the lamb's tongues over water for about 90 minutes, or until they are tender. Remove tongues. Using 250 ml (1 cup) of the "stock" made by steaming the tongues, make a sauce by adding all the remaining ingredients and simmering them together for 15 minutes. Meanwhile skin the tongues and slice or dice them. Add the tongues to the sauce, and serve over rice mixed with finely chopped fresh parsley.

*Western Cape*

## Lamb Curry

Serves 4
An economical and spicy curry that won't be too hot for anyone.

*500 g stewing lamb*
*4 potatoes*
*4 cloves garlic, crushed*
*1 piece root ginger, peeled & crushed*
*(OR 5 ml (1t) ground ginger)*
*5 ml (1t) salt*
*5 ml (1t) masala/curry powder (add more for stronger curry)*
*5 ml (1t) turmeric*
*5 ml (1t) dried origanum*
*5 ml (1t) ground cinnamon*
*2 ml (1/2t) ground cloves*
*Few black peppercorns*
*5 ml (1t) garam masala (optional)*
*30 ml (2T) ghee or oil*
*1 large onion, chopped*
*1 large tomato, peeled & chopped*
*1 whole green chilli (or red for a hotter curry)*
*250–500 ml hot water or meat stock*

Cube the meat. Peel and quarter the potatoes. Add all the flavourings and spices to the meat and stir well to coat. Heat the butter in a large saucepan and sauté the onion until golden. Add meat and stir to brown. Add the quartered potatoes, the tomato pulp and chilli and simmer, stirring gently, for a minute. Add the water stock to cover the meat, cover and cook gently until the meat is done (about 45 minutes to an hour).

Serve with rice and sambals such as these:

Mix 3 sliced bananas, 1 thinly sliced onion and 1 green chilli (seeds removed and chopped) with lemon juice, salt and a little sugar to taste.

Mix chopped cucumber, tomato and onion with lemon juice, salt and fresh coriander leaves (chopped finely).

*Transvaal*

# Frikkadels with Sour Cream Sauce

Serves 4
These meatballs of minced beef are a traditional South African favourite – the sour cream sauce gives an extremely tasty twist.

*500 g beef, minced*
*1 egg, beaten*
*125 ml (1/2 cup) milk*
*2 thick slices white bread, crusts removed*
*1 onion, chopped finely*
*5 ml (1t) dried origanum*
*5 ml (1t) salt*
*2 ml (1/2t) black pepper*
*37,5 ml (2½T) cooking oil*
*15 ml (1T) flour*
*1 × 410 g can peeled tomatoes, roughly chopped*
*2 ml (1/2t) Worcestershire sauce*
*Few drops Tabasco*
*150 ml sour cream/Smetena*

Mix the beaten egg and milk together, and pour over the slices of bread in a bowl. Leave to stand for 10 minutes to absorb the liquid, then mash with a fork. Add the beef mince, the onion, origanum, salt and pepper; mix well. With floured hands, form the mixture into even-sized patties about 5 cm in diameter. Heat the oil in a large frying pan, brown the patties quickly on both sides. Reduce heat and continue frying gently until nicely browned and cooked through.

Remove the frikkadels and drain on absorbent paper towels. Keep warm. Add the flour to the pan, stir well until brown, then add the tomatoes, Worcestershire sauce and Tabasco. Stir well and bring the sauce to the boil. Return the frikkadels to the pan, reduce heat and cover. Simmer for 5–8 minutes. Stir in sour cream and heat through. Adjust seasoning to taste and serve with rice and a green vegetable.

*Western Cape*

# Casseroled Steak with Sweet Potatoes

Serves 6
This delightful meal-in-a-dish can also be done successfully in a slow cooker or potjie. The pears are a surprising and lovely addition.

*1,5 kg stewing steak, cubed*
*45 ml (3T) cooking oil*
*45 ml (3T) butter or margarine*
*4 medium onions, chopped*
*2 ml (1/2t) dried thyme*
*Pinch ground cinnamon*
*Pinch ground cloves*
*30 ml (2T) flour*
*15 ml (1T) tomato sauce*
*1 bayleaf*
*10 ml (2t) salt*
*2 ml (1/2t) pepper*
*5 ml (1t) grated lemon rind*
*375 ml white wine*
*2 × 220 g cans pear halves*
*1 kg sweet potatoes*
*45 ml (3T) seedless raisins*
*Chopped fresh parsley for garnish*

Brown the beef cubes in the oil and butter, cooking a few at a time. Set aside. Add the chopped onion to the pot with the thyme, cinnamon and cloves, and sauté until tender. Remove from heat. Stir in flour, tomato sauce, bayleaf, salt, pepper and lemon rind. Gradually add the wine. Drain the pears, reserving 250 ml (1 cup) of the liquid. Add this liquid to the onion mixture with the browned beef cubes. Allow to simmer, covered, until the meat is tender.

Boil the sweet potatoes until tender. Peel and halve lengthwise. Add to the beef with the drained pears and the raisins. Cook uncovered till heated through and sauce is slightly thick. Sprinkle with chopped parsley before serving.

*Transvaal*

# South African Beef Casserole

(Illustrated on page 66)

Serves 6

A hearty dish with a most unusual and distinctive flavour – you can use brisket, bolo or any favourite braising beef.

*1 kg brisket of beef, sliced*
*30 ml (2T) margarine or oil*
*1 large onion, sliced*
*250 ml (1 cup) meat stock*
*60 ml (1/4 cup) wine vinegar*
*5 ml (1t) salt*
*1 bayleaf*
*5 ml (1t) caraway seed*
*Freshly ground black pepper to taste*
*4–6 Ginger Nut biscuits*

Brown the meat in the margarine or oil, using a heavy-based casserole dish on top of the stove. Pour off excess fat. Add the onion and sauté till transparent. Heat the stock, vinegar and remaining ingredients (except the biscuits) together – only add salt if your stock is not salty. Pour the mixture over the meat and onions in the casserole, cover with the lid and bake in oven preheated to 160 °C for 2 hours, or simmer on top of the stove for the same time – until the meat is very tender.

Crumble the ginger biscuits and add to the meat, stirring in well to thicken the sauce. Serve the dish hot with buttered noodles and a green salad.

*Western Cape*

# Kofta Curry

Serves 4

Meatballs in a spicy curried sauce are economical and tasty.

MEATBALLS
*250 g lean beef, minced*
*75 ml desiccated coconut*
*1 slice white bread, crumbed (no crusts)*
*15 ml (1T) turmeric*
*5 ml (1t) salt*
*2 eggs, beaten*

CURRY
*75 ml coconut soaked in 250 ml boiling water for 20*
*    minutes*
*2 onions, sliced thinly*
*15 ml (1T) oil mixed with 15 ml (1T) butter*
*15 ml (1T) lemon juice*
*45 ml (3T) very mild curry powder*
*(OR 15 ml (1T) strong curry paste)*
*250 ml (1 cup) chicken stock*
*1 apple, peeled & diced*
*2 tomatoes, peeled & chopped*
*15 ml (1T) apricot jam*
*2 cloves garlic, chopped or crushed*
*1 green chilli, whole*
*2 bayleaves*
*300 ml plain yoghurt (optional)*

Mix the meatball ingredients well (with your hands is best); the mixture will be rather sticky. Form into small meatballs (about 16) and set aside.

Pour the boiling water on the coconut and leave to "draw" milk for 20 minutes. Heat the oil and butter in a large heavy-based saucepan and sauté the onion until transparent. Mix the lemon juice with the curry powder and add to the onions. Stir and cook for a few minutes. Now add the rest of the ingredients (except the yoghurt). Strain the milk from the soaked coconut and add to the saucepan. When the liquid is boiling, add the meatballs, a few at a time. Cover the pot and leave to simmer gently until the meatballs are cooked – about 30 minutes.

Add the yoghurt and cook gently for 10 minutes more (do not boil); if the sauce needs thickening, do so with 15 ml (1T) cornflour mixed in a little water. For those who do not like cooking with yoghurt, remove the meat balls and put the sauce, onions and all, through the blender or a sieve; it will be thick and tasty; replace meatballs and heat through thoroughly. Serve the curry with plenty of rice and sambals.

*Western Cape*

# Braised Beef with Anchovies

Serves 4
A potroast brought to South Africa by Italian immigrants, in which anchovies bring out the full flavour of beef. The dish involves long, slow cooking on a coal stove – you could use a crockpot/slow cooker, to prevent the beef from burning.

*500 g beef (silverside, topside, etc)*
*1 × 50 g can of anchovies*
*2 large, juicy lemons*

Tie the piece of beef securely with string. Soak the anchovies in a little milk to reduce their saltiness; drain well before using. Cut them into small pieces and place in the pot. Add the piece of beef. (If your crockpot cannot heat meat from cold, heat the anchovies and beef in a normal pot before transferring to the heated crockpot.) Squeeze the lemons and pour the juice over. Close the lid firmly. The dish needs to cook very slowly at low heat for 3–4 hours and you should not open the pot at all during this time. Serve with vegetables.

*Transvaal*

# Boer Bobotie Pie

Serves 4–6
Bobotie in another guise – as an open pie with shortcrust pastry.

*500 g lean beef, minced*
*1 onion, chopped finely*
*15 ml (1T) cooking oil*
*15 ml (1T) curry powder/paste*
*15 ml (1T) vinegar*
*5 ml (1t) sugar*
*90 ml (6T) minced dried fruit or chutney*
*5 ml (1t) salt*
*1 slice white bread*
*200 ml milk*
*2 eggs*
*Shortcrust pastry to line 25 cm pie-dish*

Sauté the onion in the oil until transparent, then add the curry powder, meat, vinegar, sugar, dried fruit or chutney and salt. Bring to the boil, then remove from heat. Soak the bread in the milk, squeeze out (reserving the milk) and mash into the mince. Add 1 egg, beaten, and mix well.

Beat the second egg with the reserved milk (you might like to season this custard with salt and black pepper). Line a 25 cm pie-dish with shortcrust pastry rolled out about 5 mm thick. Turn the mince into the pie-dish, pour over the milk and egg, and dot with butter (optional). Bake at 200 °C for 10 minutes, then reduce heat of oven to 180 °C and bake for another 20–25 minutes or until pastry is golden and custard is set and nicely browned to taste.

Serve with chutney and salads.

*Western Cape*

## Baked Kassler Rib with Red Cabbage

Serves 4
A simple but delicious supper dish.

*4 large Kassler rib chops*
*30 ml (2T) cooking oil*
*30 ml (2T) soya sauce*
*30 ml (2T) sugar*
*30 ml (2T) wholegrain or Pommery mustard*

RED CABBAGE
*1 small red cabbage*
*30 ml (2T) cooking oil*
*1 small onion, chopped*
*2 Granny Smith apples, diced*
*2 whole cloves*
*5 ml (1t) salt*
*2 ml (1/2t) black pepper*
*15 ml (1T) vinegar*

Paint the Kassler ribs on both sides with the oil, soya sauce, sugar and French mustard mixed together into a paste. Arrange in a large ovenproof dish, cover and cook in an oven preheated to 180 °C until tender and cooked through (30–40 minutes, depending on the thickness of the chops).

Chop the red cabbage finely. Meanwhile heat the oil and sauté the onion slightly. Add the chopped cabbage and diced apples. Cover and cook on low heat for 15 minutes. Then add the cloves, salt, pepper and vinegar, and cook for another 15 minutes, adding a little water if necessary.

Serve the baked ribs on the bed of red cabbage.

*Overberg, Cape*

## Pork & Plums

Serves 4
Pork and the tartness of plums make a tasty combination. Use fresh homecooked plums if available; if you use canned plums and cannot get ones with a good colour, add a few drops of cochineal; leave a few plums whole for effect.

*4 thick pork loin chops*
*5 ml (1t) salt*
*2 ml (1/2t) pepper*
*2 ml (1/2t) dried sage or mixed herbs*
*10 ml (2t) flour*
*375 ml (1½ cups) fresh plums*
*(OR 1 × 540 g can Satsuma plums)*
*125 ml (1/2 cup) port*
*5 ml (1t) grated lemon rind*
*2 ml (1/2t) cinnamon*
*Pinch ground cloves*

Trim any fat from the chops, then season them with the salt, pepper and herbs. Flour chops lightly, and brown on both sides. Remove to a shallow buttered ovenproof dish. Drain and mash the plums, mix with the remaining ingredients and pour over the chops. (If you do not wish to use port, use 125 ml of the plum juice.) The dish may be prepared up to this stage ahead, as the flavour improves with keeping; store covered in the refrigerator (you may even store it overnight).

Bake in a moderate oven (180 °C) until tender (about 45 minutes), adding more port (or plum juice) if necessary. Serve hot with rice and a green salad.

*Natal*

# Marinated Veal Cutlets

Serves 3
Juniper berries (available bottled from delicatessens) combine with the herbs to give this dish a unique flavour. Remember that juniper berries are used to make gin!

*6 veal cutlets*
*Juice of 2 lemons*
*12 juniper berries*
*7,5 ml (1½ t) dried marjoram or thyme*
*Salt & freshly ground pepper to taste*
*15 ml (1T) butter*
*1 onion, sliced*
*125 ml (1/2 cup) white wine*
*125 ml (1/2 cup) water*
*1 carrot, sliced*

Marinate the cutlets for 1 hour in an ovenproof dish in the lemon juice, juniper berries, herbs and seasonings. In a frying pan, heat the butter and sauté the onions. Pat the cutlets dry and brown in the butter. Return cutlets to the ovenproof dish with the onion, and pour in the wine and water. Add the carrot slices. Cover with a well fitting lid and bake at 180 °C for 1–1½ hours, checking from time to time that the juices have not dried up. Serve hot with redcurrant jelly and vegetables.

*Western Cape*

# Venison Bobotie

Serves 6
A delicious variation on the theme of bobotie, very South African – and cooked just long enough not to lose the game flavour.

*1 kg pure venison mince*
*2 medium onions, chopped finely*
*30 ml (2T) butter*
*1 clove garlic, chopped or crushed*
*1 thick slice brown bread*
*250 ml (1 cup) milk*
*1 egg, beaten*
*15 ml (1T) curry paste*
*30 ml (2T) sugar*
*10 ml (2t) salt*
*2 ml (1/2t) pepper*
*2 ml (1/2t) turmeric*
*125 ml (1/2 cup) raisins*
*60 ml (4T) chutney*
*15 ml (1T) lemon juice*
*1 egg, beaten (for custard)*
*3 bayleaves*

The venison mince should not contain any fat – ask your butcher to mince a piece of venison for you. Sauté the chopped onion in the butter until golden, then add the garlic and the meat, stirring well. Fry until the meat has just coloured, then remove from heat. Soak the bread in the milk, squeeze out (reserving the milk) and mash before adding to the meat. Add all the other ingredients except the reserved milk and the final egg for the custard, and the bayleaves which are for the top of the bobotie.

Mix the meat up well and place in a buttered ovenproof dish. Roll up the bayleaves and insert into the mince so that they stand up. Bake at 180 °C for 30 minutes. Mix the reserved milk with the beaten egg and pour over the meat. Bake again at 180 °C for another 30 minutes, until topping is golden brown and set. Serve with yellow rice, chutney and sliced banana.

*Eastern Cape*

# Roast Leg of Wild Pig

Serves 6–8

Leg of wild pig is a Transvaal speciality – here it is marinated in white wine before roasting, and served with a good brown sauce.

*1 leg of wild pig*

MARINADE
*White wine & water to cover leg*
*Juice of 4 lemons*
*5 ml (1t) salt*
*5 ml (1t) ground black pepper*
*5 ml (1t) dried thyme*
*1 bayleaf*

BROWN SAUCE
*50 g bacon dripping*
*50 g bacon, chopped*
*1 large onion, chopped*
*1 large carrot, sliced*
*30 ml (2T) flour*
*500 ml (2 cups) stock*
*30 ml (2T) tomato paste*
*2 medium tomatoes, skinned & chopped*
*1 bayleaf*
*10 ml (2t) finely chopped parsley*
*4 peppercorns*
*Salt & freshly ground black pepper to taste*

Wipe the leg and marinate for 24–48 hours in enough white wine and water to cover the joint, adding the other marinade ingredients; turn the joint occasionally. (You might wish to add oil to the marinade.)

Dry the joint and roast in a medium oven (180 °C) for about 30 minutes per 500 g meat; to baste the joint, you could add wine, cider, beer or buttermilk to the pan as a moisturising flavourer for the meat (this would make a good base for a sauce afterwards).

FOR BROWN SAUCE: Heat the bacon dripping in a heavy based saucepan and add the chopped bacon, onion and carrot; cover and fry gently for 10 minutes, shaking frequently to prevent burning. Sprinkle in the flour, stir and cook over low heat (still stirring) until fat and flour turn deep gold. Remove from heat and gradually add the warmed stock. Stir over heat until sauce boils and thickens. Add the tomato paste, chopped tomatoes, bayleaf, parsley and peppercorns. Cover and simmer for 45 minutes, stirring occasionally. Strain sauce, skimming off any fat, and season to taste with salt and pepper. Reheat to serve.

Serve the roast leg of wild pig with the sauce, boiled potatoes and cabbage or other vegetables.

*Transvaal*

# Sweet-Sour Rabbit

Serves 4–6

The piquancy of French mustard adds a lovely flavour to the wine-based sauce of this excellent rabbit dish.

*2 kg rabbit, jointed*
*Salt & freshly ground black pepper*
*45 ml (3T) cooking oil*
*45–60 ml (3–4T) French mustard*
*2 onions, chopped finely*
*3 cloves garlic, crushed*
*750 ml red wine*
*5 ml (1t) dried sage*
*15 ml (1T) brown sugar*

Wipe the rabbit pieces with a cloth soaked in vinegar. Season well with salt and pepper. Heat the oil in a heavy-based casserole and sauté the joints until golden. Remove, spread with the mustard, and reserve. Add the onion and garlic to the casserole and sauté until translucent. Return the rabbit to the dish, add 250 ml (1 cup) of the wine, cover and cook for 30 minutes or until the wine has been reduced. Add the sage and sugar, then add as much of the remaining wine as needed, and simmer for another 30 minutes or until the rabbit is done.

Serve with boiled new potatoes and crusty French bread to mop up the sauce. A crisp green salad would be good on the side.

*Transvaal*

## Ostrich Fillet Sosaties in the Pan

(Illustrated on page 68)

Serves 4–8

These superb sosaties/kebabs are not for the braai – the prunes and mushrooms would burn, and ostrich fillet needs slow cooking and moisture to protect its tenderness.

*1 kg ostrich fillet*
*500 ml (2 cups) red wine*
*125 g bacon, diced*
*24 prunes*
*24 medium mushrooms*
*2 medium onions, sliced into rings*
*Salt & black pepper to taste*
*Butter or margarine for frying*

Marinate the whole pieces of ostrich fillet for 24 hours in the red wine. Drain, discarding the marinade; cut the meat into cubes. You will need 8 sosatie/kebab skewers: Thread the ostrich cubes onto them, using about 6 or 7 per skewer and alternating with the other ingredients.

Heat the butter in a large pan and fry the fillets for about 30 minutes, rotating every 10 minutes until done. Keep the sosaties warm in the oven until all are done – you could make a gravy from the pan scrapings by adding a little red wine and thickening the gravy with cornflour; a little cream would not go amiss in the sauce either!

Serve with rice and a mixed salad.

*Western Cape*

## Jugged Venison, Hare or Guinea Fowl

Serves 4

Jugged game is very tender and has a delicious sauce – but be careful not to overcook: venison breast or farm-grown guinea fowl could become too mushy as they are not generally tough. Serve with a tart jelly like quince or cranberry, or even a sweet apple jelly.

*1 kg neck, flank or breast of venison*
*(OR 1 kg jointed hare or guinea fowl)*
*1 large onion, sliced*
*4 sticks celery, chopped*
*2 bayleaves*
*6 cloves*
*12 peppercorns*
*30 ml (2T) cooking oil to brown meat*
*30 ml (2T) lemon juice*
*10 ml (2t) salt*
*2 ml (1/2t) freshly ground pepper*
*30 ml (2T) flour*
*60 ml (4T) cooking oil*
*50 ml port*

Cut the venison into neat pieces; if using hare or guinea fowl, joint and remove breast meat from the bone. Reserve all scraps and bones for the stock: Place in a saucepan, cover with about 300 ml water, add the onion, celery, bayleaves, cloves and peppercorns and simmer gently for 3 hours. Strain the stock and keep ready.

Brown the meat in 30 ml cooking oil and place in an ovenproof casserole. Pour the warm stock and the lemon juice over, adding the salt and pepper. Cover and cook in a slow oven (160 °C) for about 2½ hours. About 30 minutes before the end of cooking time, mix the flour with the 60 ml oil and a little of the stock; add to the casserole. Add the port wine, cover the casserole again, and continue cooking.

Serve with a tart red jelly, rice and vegetables. If desired, the jugged venison may be used as the filling for a game pie – when the sauce has been thickened, cool the casserole, make a good flaky or plain pastry and cover the casserole, using a pie funnel to hold up the pastry. Decorate, brush with beaten egg and bake at 200 °C, reducing the heat after the first 15 minutes.

*Eastern Cape*

# Guinea Fowl Stew

Serves 4

Note that only a tough wild bird would need to be soaked overnight in vinegar and water to tenderise it; the marinade tends to kill the unique flavour of guinea fowl if a farm-bred bird is used.

*1 guinea fowl*

MARINADE
*375 ml vinegar*
*Water*
*4 cloves*
*3 bayleaves*
*6 peppercorns*

*Ground coriander*
*Salt to taste*
*15 ml (1T) butter or good dripping*
*1 small onion, chopped*
*2 cloves garlic, chopped*
*150 g bacon or ham, chopped*
*250 ml (1 cup) hot water*
*2 cloves*
*1 bayleaf*
*4 peppercorns*
*5 ml (1t) allspice*
*125 ml (1/2 cup) red wine*
*2 ml (1/2t) sugar (optional)*
*1 × 410 g can mushroom soup*

Soak the guinea fowl overnight in the marinade (see note above – for a farm bred bird you could use a marinade of red wine and no water). Remove bird and wipe dry. Salt the bird and sprinkle with ground coriander. (The marinade is to be discarded.)

Heat the butter in a large heavy-based casserole and sauté the onion and garlic lightly. Next brown the bird for about 20 minutes. Now add the bacon or ham, the hot water and the spices, and simmer for 1 hour. When the meat is tender and almost done, add the wine and cook a little longer. Taste for seasoning – you may need salt, and the sugar is optional (it should not be necessary if the wine is reduced properly at this stage).

Cool the meat, remove the bones and cut into serving portions. Place in another casserole with the cooking liquid and the mushroom soup. Heat in the oven for about 30 minutes before the dish is to be served. Serve with rice and vegetables, and quince, guava or grape jelly.

*Eastern Cape*

# Guinea Fowl Jubilee

Serves 10–12

A guinea fowl party dish that is very sweet – but game likes sweet condiments, and the recipe is different and surprising.

*4 guinea fowl*
*Seasoned flour to coat*
*100 g butter*
*1 onion, chopped*
*125 ml (1/2 cup) raisins*
*250 ml (1 cup) chilli sauce*
*125 ml (1/2 cup) water*
*125 ml (1/2 cup) brown sugar*
*30 ml (2T) Worcestershire sauce*
*1 clove garlic, crushed*
*250 ml (1 cup) sherry*
*1 × 410 g can black cherries, drained*

Quarter the guinea fowl and shake in a bag of well seasoned flour to coat the pieces. Melt the butter in a large frying pan and brown the birds thoroughly. Place in a large, deep ovenproof casserole.

Combine the onion, raisins, chilli sauce, water, sugar, Worcestershire sauce and garlic in the frying pan that was used to brown the birds, and heat to deglaze the pan. Pour this sauce over the birds, cover and bake in the oven at 160 °C for 90 minutes. Remove lid, add the sherry and the canned cherries; bake for 15 minutes longer. Serve with rice and vegetables.

*Zululand*

# Saddle of Venison

Serves 6–8
Saddle is the finest cut of venison on the bone – it shouldn't be overcooked and may even be served pink. Saddle of springbok is preferable.

*1 small saddle venison*
*250 g spek (pork fat)*
*2 cloves garlic, crushed*
*5 ml (1t) dried mixed herbs*

MARINADE
*250 ml (1 cup) red wine*
*50 ml brown vinegar*
*50 ml water*
*2 slices lemon*
*1 carrot, sliced*
*8 peppercorns*
*1 bayleaf*
*5 ml (1t) salt*

*30 ml (2T) oil*
*1 large onion, chopped*
*Salt & freshly ground black pepper to taste*
*125 ml (1/2 cup) water*
*15 ml (1T) sweet chutney*
*Smooth apricot jam for glaze*

Remove the membrane from the meat. Cut the spek into cubes (reserving 2 thin strips) and roll the cubes in garlic and dried herbs. Scatter the spek over the joint in a deep enamelled or non-metallic dish. Mix the marinade ingredients and pour over the saddle. Refrigerate, covered, for 48 hours, turning the joint several times. Drain the meat and pat dry (reserve the marinade and spek).

Heat the oil in a large roasting pan/casserole with lid; sauté the onion. Then brown the meat lightly and season to taste with salt and pepper. Add the water, chutney and 125 ml (1/2 cup) of the marinade. Place the strips of spek on top of the joint, cover with lid and roast. (Alternately, leave out the spek strips and baste the joint at 15 minute intervals.)

The joint should be roasted for about 30 minutes per 500 g; the loins are very tender and may be served with the rosy tinge of roast beef. Cook the joint slowly, half the time with the lions down and half with bone rack down, for even cooking.

Remove the joint from the roasting pan, spread with a layer of apricot jam and place under a hot grill to glaze. Thicken the pan juices, adding extra red wine (or stock) if needed. Serve with vegetables and a red jelly.

*Natal*

# Marinating Venison

A marinade is used to tenderise or to flavour the venison – or to do both. If you do use wine, vinegar or lemon juice to tenderise, strictly speaking these are not suitable for using again in the cooking process. Vinegar and large quantities of wine will tend to make any sauce sour; if you do use the marinade in the cooking, water will have to be added to prevent the sauce being too sour. This is not as successful as the following:

Far better COOKING results are obtained from buttermilk, yogurt, cider, beer or a mixture of oil and wine. These moisturise the vension as well as flavouring it, and in addition, will reduce to a lovely sauce.

# Roast Leg of Venison

Serves 8

This recipe uses the usual lardings of spek but also a syringe to "inject" the dry venison with oil; to prevent leakage, fill the incisions with sultanas, raisins, other fruits or even finely chopped onion, producing a variety of interesting flavours.

*1 leg of venison (about 2,5 kg)*
*500 g spek to lard leg*
*6 cloves of garlic, slivered*
*250 ml (1 cup) sultanas soaked in 250 ml (1 cup) brandy*

MARINADE
*750 ml red wine*
*500 ml vinegar*
*125 ml (1/2 cup) cooking oil*
*2 onions, chopped*
*6 cloves garlic, crushed*
*4 bay leaves*
*12 black peppercorns*
*30 ml (2T) brown sugar*
*2 ml (1/2t) ground coriander*
*2 ml (1/2t) mustard powder*
*15 ml (1T) Worcestershire sauce*
*5 ml (1t) salt*

*125 ml (1/2 cup) cooking oil to inject meat*
*45 ml (3T) flour*
*5 ml (1t) salt*
*Freshly ground black pepper*
*250 g fatty bacon to cover roast*
*20 baby onions, peeled*
*20 button mushrooms*
*250 ml (1 cup) sour cream/Smetena*
*2 gherkins, finely chopped*
*2 ml (1/2t) dried mixed herbs*

Wipe venison well, and slice away all obviously dry skin and membrane. Using a sharp, slender knife or chisel, make deep incisions about 2 cm apart all over the leg, following the grain of the meat. Cut the spek into matchstick strips (these can be prepared ahead and left in the freezer to harden for easy use). Stuff each slit with a strip of spek, a couple of sultanas (these should have been soaked a good few hours, or overnight), and a sliver of garlic.

Combine the marinade ingredients in a saucepan, bring to the boil and simmer for 10 minutes; strain and leave to cool. Place leg in a large plastic bag, pour the marinade over, exhaust all air from the bag and tie tightly. Leave bagged meat in the refrigerator for 3 days, turning each morning and night. Remove from bag (reserving marinade) and wipe well to dry. Now use a hypodermic syringe to inject the cooking oil into the meat until the oil oozes out and leg is well oiled.

Dredge leg with a mixture of flour, salt and pepper. Place on a rack in a roasting pan and cover with bacon strips. Pour a little marinade into the roasting pan. Roast at 180 °C for 30 minutes, then reduce to 160 °C and roast until tender when pierced with a skewer (about 50 minutes per kilogram venison). Baste leg during this time with the marinade, every 30 minutes or so.

For the last 30 minutes of cooking, add the baby onions to the pan (these can be peeled easily after pouring boiling water over them in a bowl). For the last 10 minutes, add the button mushrooms and increase heat to 200 °C to brown the joint.

Transfer the leg, onions and mushrooms to the serving platter. Put the roasting pan on top of the stove, add the sour cream, chopped gherkins and herbs, and stir over medium heat until sauce thickens (do not allow to boil). Pour sauce over the leg, or serve separately.

For an alternate sauce: Heat 500 ml of the strained marinade until boiling and simmer until reduced and slightly thickened. Add 15 ml (1T) butter mixed to a paste with 15 ml (1T) flour, 125 ml (1/2 cup) port and 30 ml (2T) redcurrant jelly. Stir till heated through and thick.

Serve the venison with vegetables, the sauce and marula jelly on the side.

*Transvaal*

# Desserts

# Desserts

## Cold Desserts
Using Gelatine, 100

Ambrosia, 108
Avocado Cream, 98
Bavarois & Cape Gooseberries, 89
Cold Christmas Puddings, 100
Dried Fruit Compôte, 98
Fresh Fruit Terrine, 90
Fridge Cake, 109
Frozen Tropical Dessert, 99
Fruit Pizza, 94
Glace van der Hum, 106
Jewelled Cream, 109
Mango & Lime Mousse, 91
Old Fashioned Treacle Nut Pie, 97
Sinful Chocolate Mousse, 90
Strawberry Bombe, 107
Table Mountain Supreme, 106
Three-coloured Fresh Fruit Mousse, 108
Tropical Fruit Salad, 99
Valentine Meringue, 94
Van der Hum Ice Cream Cake, 107

## Hot Puddings
Brandy Pudding, 97
Butter Dumplings (Botterkluitjies), 105
Cafe Baked Bananas, 108
Caramelised Bananas, 99
Chocolate, Marmalade & Almond Bake, 89
Coffee Bread & Butter Pudding, 92
Crispy Fried Churros, 98
Grape or Peach Brandy Cream, 91
Mango Cream Cheese Meringue, 92
Marrow Charlotte, 95
"Nog 'n Skeppie" Baked Pudding, 92
Old Fashioned Sweet Dumplings (Souskluitjies), 105
Ouma Marais' Pudding, 96
Ouma's Sugar Tart, 93
Pampoenmoes, 95
Snysels (Milk Noodles), 96
Sourmilk Pudding, 95
Steamed Fruit Pudding with Cinnamon Sauce, 93

## *Bavarois and Cape Gooseberries*

(Illustrated on page 101)

Serves 10–12
A truly elegant and impressive dessert with a wonderful texture and a delicious Cape gooseberry sauce, this is well worth the effort involved.

BAVAROIS
*600 ml milk*
*4 vanilla pods or 5 ml (1t) vanilla essence*
*Pinch of salt*
*15 ml (1T) gelatine*
*60 ml (4T) hot water*
*8 egg yolks*
*200 g icing sugar, sifted*
*500 ml (2 cups) cream*

GOOSEBERRY PUREE
*500 g fresh Cape gooseberries, washed, topped & tailed*
*(OR 2 × 410 g cans Cape gooseberries, drained)*
*200 g sugar*
*2 cinnamon sticks*
*8 cloves*
*200 ml semi-sweet white wine*
*15–30ml (1–2T) gin*
*15 ml (1T) gelatine*
*60 ml (4T) hot water*

GARNISH
*300 ml fresh cream*
*Whole gooseberries for decoration*

FOR THE BAVAROIS: Break the vanilla pods into the milk in a saucepan and add the salt. Bring slowly to the boil. Add the gelatine to the water, and heat in a bowl over a saucepan of hot water. Do not allow the gelatine to boil. Beat the egg yolks with the icing sugar until frothy, then strain the milk and add it gradually to the egg yolks, whisking all the while. Place the bowl over a saucepan of hot water, or use a double boiler, and whisk until the custard thickens. (Be careful not to curdle the custard through overcooking.) Finally stir the dissolved gelatine into the custard and allow the mixture to cool until it begins to set. Whip the cream until just beginning to hold its shape, and fold into the bavarois. Chill.

FOR THE GOOSEBERRY PUREE: Bring the sugar, cinnamon, cloves and wine to the boil, add the gooseberries and

simmer slowly for 10–15 minutes in a covered saucepan over medium heat. Remove the spices and puree the fruit in a liquidiser. Add the gin. Add the gelatine to the water, and heat in a bowl over a saucepan of hot water. (Do not allow the gelatine to boil, or it will become stringy.) Stir the dissolved gelatine into the puree, then chill until just set.

TO ASSEMBLE DESSERT: Pour the bavarois into two 1-litre glass bowls and chill, then carefully spoon the gooseberry puree over. Chill well until the layers are firmly set.

GARNISH: Whip cream and pipe rosettes round the bavarois. Decorate with extra whole gooseberries.

*Natal*

## *Chocolate, Marmalade and Almond Bake*

Serves 6–8
Delicious served with whipped and brandied cream, dolloped over while the pudding is still warm.

*150 g dark chocolate*
*250 g butter*
*250 g castor sugar*
*2 eggs, separated*
*15 ml (1T) coarse-cut marmalade*
*250 g flour*
*10 ml (2t) baking powder*
*50 g ground almonds*

Melt the dark chocolate in a double boiler. Cream together the butter and sugar, add the egg yolks and the marmalade, then gradually stir in the melted chocolate. Add the flour, baking powder and ground almonds. Beat the egg whites until stiff and gently fold into the mixture. Put mixture in a loaf, ring or square cake tin or dish and bake at 180 °C for 30–40 minutes or until a tester comes out clean. Serve warm.

*Western Cape*

# Sinful Chocolate Mousse

Serves 8

Sinfully rich, this unashamedly high calorie dessert is irresistible, but then chocolate mousse is a worldwide favourite. Use the best chocolate you can afford – it makes a difference.

*250 g semisweet chocolate*
*50 ml water*
*15 ml (1T) Van der Hum, orange liqueur or brandy*
*10 ml (2t) vanilla essence*
*6 eggs (extra large), separated*
*15 ml (1T) gelatine*
*60 ml (1/4 cup) water*
*250 g butter, softened*
*2 ml (1/2t) salt*
*60 ml (4T) castor sugar*

Melt the chocolate in the water, liqueur and vanilla essence in the top of a double boiler (or in the microwave). Add the egg yolks, one at a time, beating well. Stir over heat until thick (do not allow to boil). Remove from heat. Dissolve the gelatine in the water, using a bowl over a pot of boiling water; but do not allow the gelatine to boil. Add the dissolved gelatine to the chocolate/egg mixture, stirring well. Stir in the well softened butter, little by little.

Beat the egg whites until stiff. Add the salt and the sugar 15ml at a time, still beating. Fold into the chocolate mixture, combining thoroughly. Pour into an attractive serving bowl and chill overnight until firm. To serve, decorate with cream, cherries and nuts, or with fresh strawberries, or – to compound the felony – a toffee cream liqueur.

*Transvaal*

# Fresh Fruit Terrine

(Illustrated on page 102)

Serves 8–10

A beautiful terrine of summer fruits with a mango-granadilla coulis to pour over.

TERRINE
*120 g each of 5 of the following fruits:*
*Fresh strawberries or raspberries*
*Fresh melon (e.g. spanspek), peeled & sliced*
*Pink grapefruit, in segments*
*Fresh plums, stoned & sliced*
*Fresh peaches or nectarines, sliced*
*Fresh pears, sliced*
*Granny Smith apples, sliced (with peel)*
*Black grapes, halved & seeded*
PLUS:
*2 bananas, sliced*
*1 × 10g envelope gelatine*
*6 oranges*

COULIS
*2 fresh fibreless mangoes*
*2 granadillas (or small can granadilla pulp)*

Prepare the fruit and pack all into a loaf pan or terrine to fill it. Mix the gelatine with a little water and leave to cake or "sponge". Squeeze oranges to obtain 200 ml of juice – strain this into a small saucepan and bring to the boil. Skim off the impurities as they rise, add the sponged gelatine and whisk. While still warm, pour over the fruit to cover completely. Place in refrigerator to set for at least 2 hours.

FOR THE COULIS: Peel the mangoes and remove flesh. Cut granadillas in half and remove seeds. Mix with mango flesh, liquidise and strain (unless you'd like to leave the granadilla pips in the sauce, which is slightly less elegant to look at, but tasty). Place in refrigerator.

To serve, unmould the fruit terrine onto a large elegant platter, and pour the coulis over. Or you may slice the terrine with a warmed serrated knife, place each slice on an individual plate and pour a little coulis around each slice.

*Natal*

## Grape or Peach Brandy Cream

Serves 4–6
Freestone peaches are equally good in this dessert, and less work than the grapes; or, if you are a hostess in a hurry, take a short cut and use bottled brandied peaches (see end of recipe).

*600 g seedless grapes (not too sweet)*
*(OR 6 freestone peaches)*
*Brandy to taste*
*250 ml (1 cup) cream*
*Brown sugar*

Peel the grapes (this is easier if you pour boiling water over them, then run cold water over). If they are not seedless, you will have to de-pip them. If using peaches, peel and halve, removing the pips. Place fruit in an ovenproof dish, adding brandy to moisten the fruit.

Whip the cream until soft peaks form, and flavour with brandy to taste. Pour over the fruit. Leave in the refrigerator for a few hours, until the cream is firm to the touch. Now cover with a layer of brown sugar (but don't overdo it in thickness), and place the dish under a hot grill until the sugar caramelises and trickles into the dissolving cream. (This will only take a few minutes – watch out for burning!) Serve immediately.

If you use a jar of brandied peaches, add a little of the syrup to the whipped cream for flavouring; pour the rest of the syrup over the peach halves before spreading the whipped cream over.

*Transvaal*

## Mango & Lime Mousse

Serves 6
A tangy tropical combination, with the canned mangoes imparting an excellent flavour. But you can vary the choice of fruit: fresh apricots stewed, or tinned apricots; strawberry pulp cooked with a little sugar and cooled; or dried apricots or prunes, provided they are plump and fresh-looking – soak the fruit overnight and liquidise.

*1 × 400 g can mango slices*
*1 large lime or lemon*
*3 eggs, separated*
*100 g castor sugar*
*15 ml (1T) gelatine*
*45 ml (3T) hot water*
*150 ml cream*

Drain the mango slices and puree in a liquidiser with the juice of the lime or lemon and the grated rind. Now dissolve the gelatine by moistening it with a little cold water then adding the 45 ml hot water; stir well. Allow to cool slightly.

Meanwhile beat the egg yolks with the castor sugar over boiling water until the sugar is dissolved and the mixture is light, creamy and thick. Remove from heat and add the cooled dissolved gelatine. Add the mango-lime puree. Beat the egg whites until they form soft peaks. Lightly beat the cream and fold it into the mango mixture, finally folding in the beaten egg whites – use a metal spoon or a whisk so that the mixture retains all its air.

Refrigerate for at least 1½ hours in a bowl or in individual glasses. Decorate with lime slices or sprigs of mint and cherries.

*Western Cape*

## Mango Cream Cheese Meringue

Serves 4

A quickly made dessert when mangoes are ripe and plentiful. Slimmers can use smooth cottage cheese and a sweetener.

*1 large ripe mango (about 500 g)*
*250 g smooth cream cheese, low fat*
*2 eggs, separated*
*30 ml (2T) sugar*
*Juice of half a lemon*
*30 ml (2T) almond flakes*

Peel mango and cut the flesh from the pip; cut into small cubes. Mix the cream cheese and egg yolks with 15 ml (1T) of the sugar and the lemon juice. Add the cubed mango and mix in. Pour mixture into ovenproof dish. Beat egg whites until stiff, beat in remaining sugar and spread over the cheese mixture. Sprinkle with almond flakes. Bake in an oven preheated to 200 °C for about 10 minutes, or until meringue is golden brown.

*Orange Free State*

## Coffee Bread & Butter Pudding

Serves 6

A pleasant variation on an old standby – using up not only leftover bread but coffee too!

*12 slices white bread, buttered*
*60 ml (4T) sultanas or raisins*
*125 ml (1/2 cup) strong black coffee*
*500 ml (2 cups) milk*
*250 ml (1 cup) cream*
*2 eggs*
*Pinch salt*
*30 ml (2T) sugar*
*2 ml (1/2t) vanilla essence*
*Freshly grated nutmeg*

Cut the crusts off the bread and cut each slice in half. Layer them in a greased baking dish, sprinkling each layer with sultanas. In a saucepan, heat the coffee, milk and cream to just below boiling point. Beat the eggs with the salt, sugar and vanilla and add to the milk mixture, stirring well. Pour over the bread layers and top with a good grating of fresh nutmeg.

Bake in oven preheated to 180 °C for 40 minutes.

*Transvaal*

## "Nog 'n Skeppie" Baked Pudding

Serves 6

A wonderful hot pudding for a cold night, served with a generous dollop of cream.

*1 litre milk*
*5ml (1t) bicarbonate of soda*
*45 ml (3T) butter*
*45 ml (3T) sugar*
*4 eggs, beaten*
*45 ml (3T) apricot jam*
*45 ml (3T) flour*
*Pinch salt*

Take a little of the milk to mix with the bicarbonate of soda. Set aside. Cream the butter and the sugar and add the beaten eggs. Now add the jam, flour and salt. Mix well. Add the milk gradually, and lastly the dissolved bicarbonate of soda.

Pour the mixture into a well-greased deep dish (square or round, about 23 cm across) and bake at 180 °C for 45 minutes or until golden brown and set. Serve with custard or whipped cream.

*Transvaal*

## Steamed Fruit Pudding with Cinnamon Sauce

Serves 4–6
The batter for this delicious steamed pudding must be prepared the night before.

BATTER
*250 ml (1 cup) seedless raisins*
*250 ml (1 cup) chopped dates*
*125 ml (1/2 cup) glacé cherries, quartered*
*125 ml (1/2 cup) walnuts, chopped*
*125 ml (1/2 cup) sugar*
*30 ml (2T) golden syrup*
*45 ml (3T) butter, boiled with 250 ml (1 cup) water*
*10 ml (2t) bicarbonate of soda, mixed with 250 ml (1 cup) cold water*
*500 ml (2 cups) flour, sifted*

SAUCE
*250 ml (1 cup) brown sugar*
*250 ml (1 cup) fresh cream*
*5 ml (1t) ground cinnamon*

PREPARE BATTER: Mix the fruits, nuts, sugar and syrup, then add the butter boiled with water and the bicarbonate mixed with cold water. Mix in the sifted flour and beat until bubbly. Leave the mixture to stand overnight. The next day steam in the usual way for 4 hours, OR pre-steam in open pressure cooker for 20 minutes then under pressure for 1 hour. Serve with the sauce.

FOR THE SAUCE: Stir the ingredients over low heat until the sugar dissolves and the sauce is heated through.

*Eastern Cape*

## Ouma's Sugar Tart

(Illustrated on page 103)

Serves 6
A traditional open tart – for the sweet-toothed! The brown sugar makes a jellied base underneath the milk-tart upper layer.

PASTRY
*225 g flour*
*2 ml (1/2t) salt*
*10 ml (2t) baking powder*
*150 g butter or margarine*
*1 egg, beaten*
*Cold water*

FILLING
*375 ml (1½ cups) brown sugar*
*1 egg*
*125 ml (1/2 cup) milk*
*2 ml (1/2t) vanilla essence*
*Butter*

FOR THE PASTRY: Sift together flour, salt and baking powder. Rub in the butter with your finger tips until the mixture resembles fine breadcrumbs. (You could use the food processor for this dough.) Add the egg, then enough cold water to bind dough together. Handle the dough as little as possible. Roll out to cover a large greased pie plate. (The filling will need to be shallow.)

THE FILLING: Put the brown sugar into the lined tart dish. Beat the egg in the milk, add the vanilla essence and pour it over the sugar. Dot a few lumps of butter on the tart and bake in an oven preheated to 180 °C, for about 30 minutes or until set. Serve with cream.

*Transvaal*

# Valentine Meringue

Serves 6–8
A glamorous meringue heart filled with fruit on a bed of coffee cream – sinfully rich, but ideal for a special occasion.

MERINGUE
*3 egg whites*
*140 g sugar*
*60 ml (1/4 cup) pecans or walnuts, chopped (optional)*

COFFEE CREAM
*2 egg yolks*
*100 g unsalted butter*
*30 ml (2T) sugar*
*15 ml (1T) good, strong instant coffee*
*Vanilla essence*
*60 ml (1/4 cup) pecans or walnuts, chopped (optional)*

FILLING
*250 ml (1 cup) cream*
*Fresh strawberries, hulled*
*(OR canned or brandied peaches, drained)*

FOR THE MERINGUE: Beat the whites, slowly adding the sugar until the whites stand in peaks. Fold in the nuts. Using a cooking spray, grease a sheet of foil then spoon the mixture in a large heart shape on the prepared foil. Bake in a slow oven (100 °C) for 2–3 hours, then turn off oven and leave the meringue in overnight.

COFFEE CREAM: Add the egg yolks to the well creamed butter and sugar. Mix the instant coffee with a little hot water, and add to the eggs and butter with a dash of vanilla essence to taste. Spread over the baked meringue. Sprinkle nuts over.

Whip the cream and spread over the coffee cream, then arrange the strawberries or canned peaches on the cream. Pipe more cream around if desired.

*Western Cape*

# Fruit Pizza
(Illustrated on page 104)

Serves 8–10
A summer-flavoured party dish that will earn compliments for its eye-catching appearance.

SHORTBREAD BASE
*250 g soft butter*
*125 g castor sugar*
*125 g cornflour*
*250 g cake flour*

TOPPING
*250 g cream cheese*
*50 g castor sugar*
*5 ml (1t) vanilla essence*
*Milk to mix*

FRUIT GARNISH
*Use any 5 or 6 of these fresh fruits:*
*Kiwi fruit, sliced*
*Strawberries, halved*
*Peaches or nectarines, sliced*
*Mangoes, sliced*
*Bananas, sliced*
*Litchis, sliced*
*Pineapple, thin slices quartered*
*Cherries, stoned & halved*
*Grapes, seeded & halved*
*(OR, when fresh fruit isn't available, use well drained canned fruit: mandarin segments are a must because they are so pretty; black cherries, Cape gooseberries and canned Kiwi fruit also look excellent)*

SHORTBREAD BASE: Beat the butter and castor sugar until fluffy. Add the cornflour and cake flour and mix well. Press into a greased 30 cm pizza pan. Prick well. Bake at 180 °C for 35 minutes. Cut into 8–10 slices while hot, but leave in the pan.

PREPARE TOPPING: Mix the cream cheese with the castor sugar and vanilla essence, and soften with a little milk, just sufficiently for the mixture to spread easily on the cooled baked crust. Now garnish with the fruits, arranging them in neat rings, working from the outside and alternating colours for effect. Serve before the fruits spoil or the base can turn soggy.

*Transvaal*

# Pampoenmoes

Serves 8
A traditional Cape Dutch pumpkin pudding, eaten just as often as a filling supper dish in winter.

*1 kg pumpkin, cubed*
*100 g sugar (or less to taste)*
*100 g butter*
*2 sticks cinnamon*
*125 g flour or fresh white breadcrumbs*
*Sugar & ground cinnamon mixed*

Cook the cubed pumpkin with the sugar, butter and cinnamon sticks, stirring over gentle heat until the pumpkin is soft. Remove cinnamon sticks and mash well. Stir in the flour or breadcrumbs, and continue stirring over gentle heat until the mixture has cooked through. Serve in a dish, with the sugar and cinnamon sprinkled over.

*Western Cape*

# Marrow Charlotte

Serves 4–6
A different version of the Pampoenmoes – pumpkin "mousse" – that was an old Dutch favourite. Peeled apples and rhubarb may be used in the same way, but for rhubarb omit the cinnamon.

*250 g long white marrow, weighed after peeling*
*4 slices white or brown bread, buttered*
*250 ml (1 cup) sugar*
*Ground cinnamon*
*A few whole cloves*
*250 ml (1 cup) port*

Dice the marrow flesh, removing the inside. Cut the bread into small squares. Grease a fairly deep ovenproof dish that has a lid. Alternate layers of marrow and bread, sprinkling each with sugar and cinnamon, and scattering a clove or two here and there. End up with a layer of marrow. (Fill the dish up well as it sinks considerably during baking.)

Pour the port over the pudding with the remaining sugar and cinnamon. Bake in a moderate oven (180 °C) for 1 hour, covered; then open the dish and bake another 20–30 minutes to allow pudding to brown. Serve with custard or whipped cream.

*Transvaal*

# Sourmilk Pudding

Serves 6
A traditional country way to use up sour milk, which is thick and pleasantly tart in flavour. In the city, cultured buttermilk should be substituted.

*500 ml (2 cups) sour milk, or buttermilk*
*250 ml (1 cup) fresh milk*
*250 ml (1 cup) sugar*
*125 ml (1/2 cup) butter*
*2 eggs*
*250 ml (1 cup) selfraising flour*

Mix the sour milk or buttermilk with the fresh milk. Cream the sugar, butter and eggs well together. (This can be done in the processor.) Add the milk mixture. Then add the flour slowly, stirring by hand to mix in well. Pour batter into a greased ovenware dish and bake in a medium oven (180 °C) for about 45 minutes or until golden brown on top. Delicious served with stewed fruit such as quinces.

*Western Cape*

## Ouma Marais' Pudding

Serves 6–8
A satisfying pudding – serve it hot, with Cassia Custard (see below), or in summer serve it cold with Summer Cream.

*80 ml (1/3) cup Pronutro Great Start granules*
*125 g butter*
*500 ml (2 cups) sugar*
*2 ml (1/2t) salt*
*4 eggs, separated*
*60 ml (4T) flour*
*500 ml (2 cups) milk*
*Juice & zest of 2 large lemons*

CASSIA CUSTARD
*500 ml (2 cups) milk*
*50 g custard powder*
*30 ml (2T) yellow sugar*
*30 ml (2T) cream*
*2 ml (1/2t) vanilla essence*
*Stick of cassia bark (or cinnamon)*
*2 ml (1/2t) lemon rind, grated*
*1 clove*
*Freshly ground nutmeg*

For the Pronutro granules you may substitute any granola type cereal, or even toasted brown breadcrumbs. Cream the butter, sugar and salt together, then add the Pronutro granules, the egg yolks, flour, milk and the lemon juice and zest. Beat the egg whites until stiff, then fold into the mixture.

Pour mixture into an ovenproof dish, place it in a roasting pan with hot water to come at least halfway up the sides, and bake at 180 °C for about 1 hour, by which time the top should be browned and the base firm to the touch.

CASSIA CUSTARD: Bring the milk to the boil. Mix the custard powder, sugar, cream and vanilla essence to a paste in a bowl. Add a little of the hot milk to the paste and stir till smooth. Now add the thinned paste to the milk in the saucepan, turning down the heat and stirring in the cassia stick (use cinnamon if you have no cassia), lemon rind, clove and nutmeg. Simmer, stirring constantly, until custard is thick and creamy. Remove the cassia stick. Serve the custard warm or cooled, with Ouma Marais' Pudding.

In summer, you might prefer to serve the dessert cold, with SUMMER CREAM: 250 ml (1 cup) cream whipped and flavoured with 15 ml (1T) icing sugar and a few drops rose essence (available from pharmacists).

*Western Cape*

## Snysels (Milk Noodles)

Serves 4
A traditional Cape Dutch dessert, in which homemade ribbon noodles are cooked in milk and served with cinnamon or nutmeg – snysels were a favourite supper dish for children.

*250 ml (1 cup) flour*
*1 litre milk*
*250 ml (1 cup) sugar*
*Stick of cinnamon*
*3 cardamom seeds*
*Pinch salt*

Mix the flour with sufficient cold water to make a pliable dough; knead well on a floury surface. Still using plenty of flour, roll out the dough until almost paper thin. Use a sharp knife to cut thin noodles, using more flour to keep them separate.

Bring the milk and the other ingredients to the boil in a heavy bottomed saucepan. Add the flour noodles. Simmer over low heat for about 30 minutes until thick and creamy. Serve hot, with ground cinnamon or nutmeg sprinkled over.

*Western Cape*

# Old Fashioned Treacle Nut Pie

Serves 6
Good quality pecan nuts are grown in this country and are widely available. Fresh pecans make an attractive and irresistible pie.

*125–250 ml (1/2–1 cup) pecan nut halves*

PASTRY
*250 ml (1 cup) flour*
*5 ml (1t) baking powder*
*15 ml (1T) sugar*
*125 g butter*

TREACLE FILLING
*2 eggs, separated*
*125 ml (1/2 cup) golden syrup*
*30 ml (2T) treacle or molasses*
*30 ml (2T) cornflour, dissolved in little water*
*250 ml (1 cup) water*
*15 ml (T) butter*
*2 ml (1/2t) vanilla essence*

Make the pastry case ahead (the mixing can be done in the processor): Sift flour and baking powder, add sugar then rub in butter until dough is like crumbs. Press into greased pie dish and bake at 180 °C for about 10 minutes. Arrange the pecan nut halves on the pastry, before pouring the treacle filling over.

TREACLE FILLING: Mix together the lightly beaten egg yolks, the syrup and treacle, cornflour, water and butter in a saucepan. Beat with a whisk over moderate heat until the sauce thickens. Add the vanilla essence, and fold in the stiffly beaten egg whites. Pour over the nuts in the pie case. Bake at 180 °C until set (about 30 minutes). Remove from oven to cool before serving, with cream on the side.

*Western Cape*

# Brandy Pudding

Serves 6
Rich and tipsy, this is a favourite South African dessert.

*150 g pitted dates*
*250 ml (1 cup) boiling water*
*5 ml (1t) bicarbonate of soda*
*125 g butter*
*200 g sugar*
*2 eggs, beaten*
*200 g flour*
*1 ml (1/4t) baking powder*
*2 ml (1/2t) salt*

BRANDY SAUCE
*100 g sugar*
*15 ml (1T) butter*
*250 ml (1 cup) water*
*100 ml brandy*
*5 ml (1t) vanilla essence*

Pour the boiling water and bicarbonate of soda over the dates in a bowl; set aside to cool. Cream the butter and sugar; add the eggs. Sift the flour, baking powder and salt into the butter/egg mixture and mix well. Add the dates and their liquid and stir well. Pour into a greased ovenproof dish that is deep enough to contain the baked pudding and still allow for the Brandy Sauce to be poured over afterwards. Bake at 180 °C for 35 minutes. Turn off the oven but leave the pudding in the heat; prick the pudding for penetration, then pour the prepared sauce over.

BRANDY SAUCE: Heat the sugar, butter and water in a saucepan and stir to dissolve sugar thoroughly; remove from the heat and add the brandy and vanilla essence. Pour immediately over the pudding in the oven, and leave to stand in the warmth for a while for the full flavour to develop. Serve with cream.

*Transvaal*

## Avocado Cream

Serves 12
A rich, smooth avocado fool that can equally well be
frozen and served as a gourmet ice cream.

*3 medium avocados*
*250 ml (1 cup) milk*
*250 ml (1 cup) sugar*
*125 ml (1/2 cup) fresh lemon juice*
*5 ml (1t) vanilla essence*
*500 ml (2 cups) thick cream*
*15 ml (1T) roughly grated lemon rind*

Peel the avocados and cube the flesh. Place in the
blender or processor with the milk, sugar, lemon juice
and vanilla essence. Process until smooth, then pour
into a large bowl. Whip the cream until thick, then
(reserving a little for decoration) fold it into the avocado
puree.

(For a slightly firmer cream, use 10 ml gelatine, used
to your favourite method. This should be added to the
mixture before the whipped cream. However, do not
use gelatine if you intend to freeze the dessert.)

Pour into one large dish or 12 small dishes or glasses.
Chill. To serve, decorate with the reserved cream and
grated lemon rind.

*Eastern Cape*

## Crispy Fried Churros

Makes 12
Spanish-style treats fried and dipped in icing sugar –
delicious with hot chocolate.

*250 g flour*
*5 ml (1t) salt*
*450 ml water*
*Oil for deep frying*
*Icing sugar to dust churros*

Sift the flour and salt together. Bring the water to the
boil in a medium sized saucepan. Remove from the heat
and pour in the flour, beating with a wooden spoon
until the mixture forms a thick paste that pulls away
from the sides of the saucepan. Cool to room temperature.

Heat a few centimetres of oil in a deep frying pan
until hot but not smoking. Spoon half the dough into a
biscuit/cookie press or piping bag, with a star nozzle,
and press out about 15 cm of dough at a time, forming a
coil directly into the hot oil. (If you do not have a biscuit
press, shape small dumplings by hand.) Fry, turning,
until the churro is golden brown all over (about 5–7
minutes); place on absorbent paper to drain. Continue
until dough is used up. Dust the churros with icing sugar
(or plain sugar) and serve while fresh and warm.

*Transvaal*

## Dried Fruit Compôte

Serves 4-6
Dried fruit is one of South Africa's best products; experi-
ment with different flavours for this simple but refreshing idea. Choose plump, moist-looking fruits and use the
best of the pure fruit juices on sale.

*500 g dried fruit (e.g. pears or apricots)*
*500 ml–1 litre pure fruit juice (pear or apricot, etc.)*

Place the dried fruit, which you may prefer to cut up, in
a large covered container or glass jar with screw top.
You must allow room for the fruit to expand as it
absorbs the fruit juice. Now pour a suitable choice of
pure fruit juice over the fruit to cover, and leave to stand
at room temperature for 12 hours or so, topping up
with fruit juice as necessary.

Chill before serving with cream, custard or plain
yoghurt. You might like to blend the fruit and its juices
to a puree to serve with cream or ice cream. (Note: The
compôte is also good as a breakfast dish with cereal.)

*Western Cape*

# Tropical Fruit Salad

Serves 6–8
A good fruit salad is part of the South African tradition – this one mixes many tropical flavours.

*6 bananas*
*Few litchis (optional)*
*6 guavas*
*4 large peaches*
*4 small fibreless mangoes*
*6 kiwi fruit*
*1 small Queen pineapple*
*Pulp of 6 granadillas*
*Juice of 1 Cape lemon & 2–3 oranges*
*(OR 60 ml (1/4 cup) Van der Hum liqueur)*

Peel and slice bananas and litchis, and sprinkle with lemon juice to prevent discolouration. Peel and slice the rest of the fruit into the bowl, and mix the granadilla pulp with the lemon and orange juice (or Van der Hum). Pour over the mixed fruit in the bowl and leave for several hours to allow the flavour to blend. Chill in the refrigerator overnight or until needed. Serve with cream, custard or ice cream.

*Transvaal*

# Frozen Tropical Dessert

Serves 4
A rich ice cream laden with tropical fruits – a South African cassata to make at home.

*1 large avocado*
*1 × 400 g can peach slices, drained*
*180 ml (2/3 cup) grated pineapple*
*60 ml (1/4 cup) chopped dates*
*12 maraschino cherries*
*125 g smooth cream cheese*
*200 ml cream*
*30 ml (2T) lemon juice*
*30 ml (2T) castor sugar*

Peel and slice the avocado thinly, or dice. Dice the peach slices and grate the pineapple (if using canned pineapple, shred). Remove pits and chop dates. Halve the maraschino cherries.

Cream the cheese, adding 60 ml (4T) of the cream gradually; stir until smooth. Add lemon juice and sugar. Whip the ramaining cream until thick and fold into the cream cheese mixture. Combine carefully with the prepared fruits. Pour into the freezing tray of the refrigerator and freeze until firm. Serve each portion decorated with a rosette of whipped cream flavoured with liqueur.

*Eastern Cape*

# Caramelised Bananas

Serves 4
Bananas in citrus juices, caramelised to eat with ice cream – a simple and fairly economical but not low kilojoule dessert!

*8 bananas*
*50 g butter*
*80 g sugar*
*250 ml (1 cup) fresh orange juice*
*30 ml (2T) fresh lemon juice*

Heat the butter in a frying pan or, for the microwave, a shallow glass dish. Slice the bananas (in rings or lengthwise) into the heated butter and cook for a few minutes. (Coat the slices by turning them in the butter.)

Remove the banana slices, add the sugar to the butter and heat strongly until it browns, stirring (for the microwave, once each minute for 3 minutes). In the frying pan, first add the banana slices, turning constantly and cooking for 2 minutes; then add the orange and lemon juice (these must be freshly squeezed), and stir for another minute before serving. For the microwave, add the juice first and stir; microwave for 5 minutes, then add the banana slices and heat for another 2 minutes.

Serve the banana slices over ice cream, or with whipped cream for special occasions.

*Transvaal*

## Cold Christmas Pudding

Serves 6–8
The ideal Christmas pudding for our hot climate. The chocolate and marshmallows are easily and quickly melted in the microwave.

*60 ml (1/4 cup) citron or mixed peel, finely cut*
*125 ml (1/2 cup) preserved ginger, finely cut*
*125 ml (1/2 cup) glacé cherries, chopped finely*
*250 ml (1 cup) dates, stoned & chopped finely*
*125 ml (1/2 cup) currants*
*125 ml (1/2 cup) chopped nuts*
*2 ml (1/2t) salt*
*45 ml–125 ml brandy (to taste)*
*30 ml (2T) gelatine*
*125 ml (1/2 cup) boiling water*
*625 ml (2½ cups) milk*
*250 g dark chocolate*
*250 g marshmallows*
*1 packet Orley Whip*
*(OR 250 ml (1 cup) cream)*

Prepare the fruits and nuts and mix in a large jar or container with a lid. Add the salt, and brandy to taste, to moisten the fruits. Cover and leave in the refrigerator for a week, shaking the jar daily to encourage absorption.

Dissolve the gelatine in the boiling water. Place the milk in a saucepan, break in the chocolate and add the marshmallows. Stir constantly over low heat until all has melted to a smooth cream (this is easily done in the microwave). Remove from heat and add the dissolved gelatine, stirring well. Now add the brandied fruit and nuts. Leave the mixture to cool in the fridge until half set. Beat the Orley Whip (or you can substitute cream) until stiff. Fold gently into the fruit mixture. (At this stage you may add sterilised coins.)

Pour into a lightly oiled ring mould – you may wish to add extra cherries to the base, so that they will appear on top of the pudding when it is unmoulded. Cover dessert with oiled wax paper and refrigerate overnight. To unmould, run heated knife round the edge of the dessert and turn onto chilled serving platter. Decorate with glacé fruit and holly if desired. Serve with ice cream. (This is a light coloured dessert, but a welcome change at Christmas in our climate.)

*Overberg, Cape*

## Using Gelatine

Gelatine often frightens people but it shouldn't – it's easy when you know how to use it.

You can try the method given on the packet.

Or take a small container with the measured amount of COLD water (it is vital that it should be cold). Sprinkle the measured gelatine over the surface of the water (or other liquid), shaking constantly until it has been absorbed. Do NOT stir.

Leave for approximately 1 minute until the mixture has "caked" or "sponged" – this means that the mixture has turned into a solid cake. Then either place over the lowest heat on top of the stove until the mixture has turned tranparent but hasn't boiled, OR microwave on medium power until transparent but not boiling. The timing depends on the microwave but for the first time start by setting the timer to 35 seconds.

Add to the mixture that requires the gelatine's setting action.

*Opposite:* A truly stunning dessert, Bavarois with Cape Gooseberries, dominates this category
*Overleaf: (left)* Fresh Fruit Terrine; and *(right)* Ouma's Sugar Tart – reflecting today's cuisine and the traditions of our past
*Page 104:* Fruit Pizza, shown here with a choice of beautiful canned fruits on the shortbread base
*Prepared with choice ingredients from Woolworths food markets*

# Old Fashioned Sweet Dumplings (Souskluitjies)

Serves 4

Cinnamon flavoured dumplings, a Dutch favourite from the South African past.

DUMPLINGS
*250 ml (1 cup) flour*
*10 ml (2t) baking powder*
*Pinch salt*
*15 ml (1T) butter or margarine*
*2 eggs, beaten*
*125 ml (1/2 cup) milk*
*Cinnamon & sugar*

SYRUP
*125 ml (1/2 cup) water*
*125 ml (1/2 cup) golden syrup or sugar*
*15 ml (1T) butter*
*2 cloves*
*15 ml (1T) sweet sherry*

FOR THE DUMPLINGS: Sift the dry ingredients together and rub in the butter; mix well with the beaten eggs and milk. (This can all be done in the processor.) Submerge teaspoons of the mixture into boiling, lightly salted water. Cover the pot and simmer dumplings gently for 15 minutes. Remove with a slotted spoon, drain and place in ovenproof dish sprinkled with cinnamon. Sprinkle more cinnamon and a little sugar over the dumplings. Keep warm.

When all the dumplings have been made, prepare the SYRUP: Use water from cooking the dumplings; boil the ingredients up until the sugar has dissolved and pour over the dumplings in the dish. Place in a low oven to keep warm until needed.

*Orange Free State*

# Butter Dumplings (Botterkluitjies)

Serves 4-6

These equally traditional sweet dumplings are a little more trouble to make, but are melting, rich and utterly delicious.

*3 eggs, separated*
*500 ml (2 cups) milk*
*5 ml (1t) baking powder*
*45 ml (3T) cornflour*
*Pinch salt*
*250 ml (1 cup) melted butter*
*Cinnamon & sugar mixed*

Beat the egg yolks. Separately beat the egg whites until stiff. Heat the milk in a large saucepan. Mix the baking powder, cornflour and salt with the beaten egg yolks, and add this to the milk as it begins to boil. Stir the mixture thoroughly and cook over slightly lowered heat until the cornflour and eggs are cooked, and the mixture is thick. Remove from the heat and fold in the beaten egg whites.

Dip a dessertspoon in the melted butter and scoop out a dumpling from the mixture; place in an ovenproof dish. Repeat until you have a complete layer of dumplings; now scatter them with cinnamon and sugar. Repeat until all the mixture has been used.

Now fill the cup of melted butter with boiling water and pour this over the layered dumplings. Warm through in the oven before serving.

*Western Cape*

# Table Mountain Supreme

Serves 12
A light, delectable trifle made to resemble Table Mountain with its white cloth – a family recipe that was once served at elegant Cape Town dinner parties.

SPONGE CAKE
*5 eggs (extra large)*
*250 ml (1 cup) sugar*
*45 ml (3T) dry white wine*
*250 ml (1 cup) flour*
*5 ml (1t) baking powder*

WINE SAUCE
*9 eggs, separated (extra large)*
*750 ml dry white wine*
*15 ml (1T) vanilla essence*
*250 ml (1 cup) sugar*
*250 ml (1 cup) pineapple juice (from can below)*

FRUIT FILLING
*1 × 500 g can pineapple chunks*
*1 × 200 g can cherries, pitted*
*1 × 500 g can pie apples*

*250 ml (1 cup) almonds, sliced (with skins)*
*9 egg whites (from Wine Sauce eggs)*

Starting the day before, bake the SPONGE CAKE: In an electric mixer or processor, beat the eggs and sugar until thick and lemon-coloured. Add the wine and beat a few minutes more. Sift the flour and baking powder and add to the mixture, mixing in well but no longer beating. Line the base of a 22 cm springform cake tin with greased wax paper. Pour the batter into the tin and bake at 180 °C for 30 minutes or until done. Remove from oven and allow to cool before running a knife round the cake and releasing it. Carefully peel off the paper.

Drain the fruit for the filling well, reserving the pineapple juice to use in the WINE SAUCE: Stir the egg yolks, wine, vanilla, sugar and pineapple juice together in the top of a double boiler over hot (not boiling) water. Cook gently, stirring constantly until the sauce thickens and coats the spoon. (The sauce will however be of a fairly thin consistency overall.) Allow to cool.

TO ASSEMBLE: Cut the cake's rounded edges off to form a square, reserving the rounded pieces. Cut the squared cake in two and lay one half in an ovenproof serving dish. Scatter with half the fruit filling, pour some of the wine sauce over and sprinkle a quarter of the sliced almonds on top. Now place the other half of the cake on top, repeating the scattering of fruit and pouring more wine sauce over the "mountain". Add the rounded slices at both ends to resemble Table Mountain and pour the remaining wine sauce over to hold all together.

Beat the egg whites until stiff and dry. (Do not add any sugar.) Use a spatula to coat the cake with the egg whites. Scatter the remaining almonds along the bottom reaches of the "mountain".

Bake at 130 °C for 10 minutes – just long enough to dry the egg whites. Now place a piece of foil on the top of the cake to prevent the "tablecloth" from browning. Bake for another 10 minutes until the bottom is a light brown, while the top remains white. The meringue should resemble the cloud on Table Mountain, while the almonds imitate its stony footholds. Turn off the heat and leave the cake in the oven for 1 hour. Remove from oven and cool to room temperature.

TO SERVE: Allow your guests to take scoops of Table Mountain, as if it were a trifle. Rich and delicious!

*Transvaal*

# Glace van der Hum

Serves 4–6
Ice cream with Van der Hum liqueur and nuts.

*500 ml (2 cups) cream*
*4 egg yolks*
*200 ml Van der Hum liqueur*
*125 ml (1/2 cup) pecan nuts, crushed*
*15 ml (1T) castor sugar*

Whip the cream until thick, then add the egg yolks, still beating constantly. Now add the liqueur, nuts and sugar; mix well. Place in the freezer for 1 hour. Remove from freezer and whip the partially frozen ice cream again. Replace in freezer until needed.

*Natal*

# Van der Hum Ice Cream Cake

Serves 6–8
An ice cream cake flavoured with that most South African of liqueurs, Van der Hum – an old Cape speciality redolent with spices and naartjie (tangerine) peel.

*500 ml (2 cups) cream*
*1 × 395 g can condensed milk*
*4 eggs, separated*
*5 ml (1t) gelatine*
*15 ml (1T) boiling water*
*60 ml (4T) Van der Hum liqueur*

GARNISH
*125 ml (1/2 cup) cream*
*1 egg white (from above eggs)*
*15 ml (1T) castor sugar*
*Segments of fresh naartjie/tangerine*

Combine 125 ml (1/2 cup) of the cream with the condensed milk and the yolks of the 4 eggs. Cook over hot water, or in a double boiler, stirring constantly until the mixture coats the back of the spoon. Dissolve the gelatine in the boiling water and add to the custard. Remove from heat and allow to cool, stirring to prevent a skin from forming. Leave until completely cold.

Now stir in the liqueur. Beat the other 250 ml of the cream until it holds its shape; beat 3 of the 4 egg whites until very stiff. Fold both into the custard mixture, and pour into a springform cake tin or Tupperware mould. Place in the freezer and leave until firm – do not beat during this time. To turn out, hold a cloth wrung in warm water round the cake tin for 1–2 minutes; invert tin over a serving platter.

FOR GARNISH: Whip the cream until it holds its shape; beat the egg white till stiff, then add the castor sugar and beat until it is incorporated. Fold the cream into the egg white. Pipe onto the unmoulded cake and return to the freezer. (At this stage, you may keep the dessert for up to 2 months.) Allow to thaw a little in the refrigerator before serving, complete with the naartjie/tangerine segments. (If there are no fresh fruits, you may use drained mandarin orange segments.)

*Western Cape*

# Strawberry Bombe

Serves 12
A festive dessert made a day ahead and unmoulded hopefully to cries of appreciation from your guests!

INGREDIENTS
*5 punnets fresh strawberries*
*Castor sugar to taste*
*75 ml Kirsch, Cointreau or other liqueur*
*1 litre cream (4 × 250 ml cartons)*
*4 packets Boudoir (finger) biscuits*
*Milk or water*

METHOD
Wash and then mash the strawberries (reserving 1 punnet for decoration); add sugar to taste, then the liqueur. Whip 750 ml of the cream until firm. Now line a suitable large bowl with the finger biscuits, dipping each quickly into cold milk or water first. Spoon in a layer of the strawberry mix; then a layer of whipped cream; then a layer of finger biscuits (dry this time). Continue until the bowl is filled, ending with a layer of biscuits. Refrigerate overnight until firm.

To unmould, dip bowl into warm water and invert onto serving platter. Whip the remaining 250 ml cream and use to decorate the Bombe, with the reserved whole strawberries.

*Transvaal*

## Café Baked Bananas

Serves 2
A quickly made treat to serve with ice cream or cream –
double up for more helpings.

*2 bananas*
*125 ml (1/2 cup) strong filter coffee*
*125 ml (1/2 cup) Kahlua/coffee liqueur*
*45 ml (3T) brown sugar (optional)*

Peel bananas and slice in half lengthways – place in
greased ovenproof dish. Mix the black coffee and liqueur
with the sugar (to taste) and pour over the bananas.
Bake at 180 °C for 20 minutes. Serve over ice cream or
with cream.

*Transvaal*

## Ambrosia

Serves 6–8
A beautiful fruit dessert with a dressing of honey and
liqueur to make it memorable. Any lovely fruit in season
could be used.

*1 large fibreless mango*
*500 g seedless grapes*
*10 litchis*
*5 nectarines*
*4 pieces watermelon konfyt/preserve*
*4 pieces crystallised ginger*

HONEY LIQUEUR DRESSING
*30 ml (2T) honey*
*30 ml (2T) fresh lemon juice*
*30 ml (2T) liqueur, eg Van der Hum*

Peel fruit and slice or cut finely into an attractive glass
bowl. (Note: Alternatives are strawberries, kiwi fruit,
pears or bananas. Each fruit must be ripe and choice of
its kind.) Slice the watermelon konfyt and ginger very
thinly and add to the salad.

DRESSING: Mix the ingredients, warming them slightly
if the honey is very stiff. Pour over the salad and toss
gently. Chill thoroughly.
    Decorate the salad with blue borage flowers or sprigs
of fresh mint, and serve with whipped cream.

*Western Cape*

## Three-coloured Fresh Fruit Mousse

Serves 6–8
A pretty dessert that can be made all year round from a
selection of different coloured fruits. Below is a summer
choice of fruits – start the dessert the day before it is
needed.

*500 g peaches or nectarines*
*500 g kiwi fruit or green melon*
*500 g strawberries*
*3 packets jelly (yellow, green, red)*
*Boiling water*
*500 ml (2 cups) cream*

METHOD
Peel and slice the peaches or nectarines into the blender
or processor, and process until smooth. Dissolve half the
yellow jelly powder in 125 ml (1/2 cup) boiling water,
add a third of the cream, and add to the fruit in the
processor; process for a minute. Pour into an attractive
glass bowl as the bottom layer, and leave in the refrigerator until firmly set.
    Peel and slice the kiwi fruit or melon and make the
green mousse layer with half the green jelly and a third
of the cream, in the same way as for the first layer.
Leave to set firm. Repeat with the strawberries and the
red jelly, using the rest of the cream. When all three
layers are set, decorate with fresh fruit and nuts, and
extra cream if desired.

*Overberg, Cape*

# Jewelled Cream

Serves 10–12

A moulded iced dessert made up of mixed crystallised fruits. If you wish to use it as a frozen Christmas pudding, add a little liqueur for a festive flavour.

*50 g each of these crystallised fruits:*
*Figs*
*Orange*
*Pineapple*
*Melon*
*Pear*
*Peach*
*Ginger*
*Glacé cherries (red)*
*Glacé cherries (green)*
*125–250 ml sweet white wine*

CUSTARD CREAM
*3 egg yolks*
*100 g castor sugar*
*30 g flour*
*300 ml milk*
*250 ml (1 cup) cream*

Dice the crystallised fruits and soak overnight in sweet white wine to cover. Drain thoroughly.

CUSTARD CREAM: Beat the egg yolks with the sugar and flour. Bring the milk to the boil and pour into the egg mixture in a bowl, beating well until smooth. Using a double boiler, heat the custard and stir until very smooth and thick. Cool. Beat the cream until just forming peaks, then gently fold into the cooled custard.

Fold the drained fruits into the Custard Cream and pour into a bowl or mould; place in the freezer until firm. (Obviously the dessert will keep for a long time in the freezer, if required. But once you have thawed the dessert, it is best not to re-freeze it.)

To serve, unmould and/or defrost until just turning soft.

*Natal*

# Fridge Cake

Serves 12

Rich and flavoursome but not too sweet – a no-bake fridge cake that makes a pleasant dessert with ice cream and a little liqueur.

*3 packets Marie biscuits*
*250 ml (1 cup) walnuts (optional)*
*250 g butter or margarine, softened*
*250 g sugar*
*60 ml (4T) cocoa powder*
*5 ml (1t) vanilla essence*
*4 eggs*

You will probably need only 2½ of the packets of Marie biscuits (about 500 g) to add to the boiled mixture; break them into a large bowl, and add the nuts when you are feeling lavish or it is a special occasion.

First cream the butter and sugar well (this can be done in the processor). Sift the cocoa powder into the mixture, then the vanilla; mix well. Use a double boiler, or a saucepan with a heavy base and bring the mixture to the boil slowly, stirring constantly. The mixture will turn pale brown, then will gradually darken and thicken. (Be careful not to burn it.) When it is deep brown and still smooth, remove from heat and allow to cool slightly; now add the eggs one at a time and beat in well.

Pour the mixture over the broken biscuits in the bowl. Mix swiftly and vigorously with a stout wooden spoon; despite initial appearancess, the biscuits will not be too much for the mixture.

Have ready two loaf tins or a large square cake tin, greased and lined with wax paper (so that you can lift the chilled cake out of the tin easily). Pour the mixture into the lined tins and press down hard and well into the corners. The cake should be smooth and compacted. When cool, place in the refrigerator and leave overnight or longer. (The cake keeps well in the fridge, but not out of it.)

Cut into slices or squares and serve with ice cream and liqueur as a special dessert.

*Western Cape*

# Index

(For purely alphabetical listings of recipe titles,
consult the section index for Starters, Salads, etc)

*The recipes in this book came from:*

STARTERS: Diane Cardell, Durban; André Clark, Koffiefontein; Mrs L Clark, Kloof; Susan Coetzee, Cape Town; Wendy de Lorm, Orchards; Mrs PB Edwards, Cramerview; Mrs L Fourie, Athlone; H Glennie, Somerset East; Henriëtte Hugo, Bonnievale; Cynthia Koning, Parow; Rae Labuschagne, Irene; Bianca Lawrence, Pietermaritzburg; Jean McAllan, Cathcart; Marian McQueen, Cowies Hill; Helen Murchison, Craighall Park; Jenni Rabinowitz, Constantia; Mrs J Roux, Port Elizabeth; Linda Sandilands, Krugersdorp North; Adele Seady, Port Elizabeth; Annette Truter, Port Alfred; A Walker, Pietermaritzburg; Gail Warren, Hillcrest

SALADS: Robyn Arnold, Murrayfield; Christine Carter, Camps Bay; Louise Chalmers, Bedfordview; Norma Coetzee, Stellenbosch; Mrs S Coston, Rosettenville; Fay Engelbrecht, Parkhurst; C Handley, Gardenview; MJ Kibble, Port Elizabeth; Cynthia Koning, Parow; Bianca Lawrence, Prestbury; Joan Lipp, Bergvliet; Jean McAllan, Cathcart; Ann Nairn, Pinetown; Mrs J Roux, Port Elizabeth; Linda Sandilands, Krugersdorp North; Emile Shreve, Three Anchor Bay; Mrs A Southey, Cedarville; Mavis Toms, Wierda Park; Elsa Vorster, Stellenbosch; Gail Warren, Hillcrest

FISH & SEAFOOD: Ann Bass, Winterton; June Blake, Durban; Paddy Briant, Simon's Town; Jane Chester, Albertville; André Clark, Koffiefontein; Mrs M Darlington, Lyttelton; David Fig, Claremont, Cape; H Glennie, Somerset East; Fern Hawksworth, Bothasig; Mrs CJ Higgo, Voëlklip; Joan Jooste, Plumstead; Mrs C Landau, Cape Town; Bianca Lawrence, Pietermaritzburg; Roma Lewis, Klerksdorp; Mrs B Maltz, Sea Point; Jenni Rabinowitz, Constantia; Zuretha Roos, Linden; Hazel Taute, George; Annette Truter, Port Alfred; YD Watson, Mbabane

OUTDOOR COOKING: Lizelle Bright, Malvern; Mrs L Clark, Kloof; Norma Coetzee, Stellenbosch; Mrs M Craig, Transvaal; Ann Eckley, Paulshof; Mrs PB Edwards, Cramerview; Eliza Fuller, Edgemead; Mrs H Holzhausen, Germiston; Yvette Horvitch, Johannesburg; Bianca Lawrence, Prestbury; Rowan Mentis, Bedfordview; Susan Rawlings, Sasolburg; Zuretha Roos, Linden; Mrs J Roux, Port Elizabeth; Annette Truter, Port Alfred; Val Winstanley, Benoni

MEAT, GAME & CHICKEN: E Armour, Hermanus; Mrs Bernardi, Krugersdorp; Sheila Black, Hluhluwe; P Buchanan, Pretoria; Mrs EM Cameron, Port Elizabeth; Mrs L Clark, Kloof; Fern Hawksworth, Bothasig; Mrs J Kemp, Tylden; Rosemary Kets, Camps Bay; R Kholvadia, Klerksdorp; Cynthia Koning, Parow; Betty Lotter, Mooinooi; Mrs B Maltz, Sea Point; Mario Nero, Pietermaritzburg; Deborah O'Reilly, Somerset West; CD Pope, Claremont, Cape; Chick Power, Bergvliet; Zuretha Roos, Linden; JF Steinhobel, Houghton; Freda Stevens, Northlands; Annette Truter, Port Alfred; N Twidale, Newlands, Cape; Elsa Vorster, Stellenbosch; A Walker, Pietermaritzburg; Gail Warren, Hillcrest; Mrs MF Watson, Port Elizabeth; Mrs R Wemyss, Howick

DESSERTS: E Armour, Hermanus; Mrs R Bernstein, Bramley; Mrs LC Bonell, Hartebeespoort; Yvonne Collett, Kensington, Tvl; Sue Cowley, Melkbosstrand; Ursula Crossley, Fouriesburg; Edna Davis, Durban North; Astri de Villiers, Camps Bay; Mrs M de Villiers, Somerset West; Mrs PB Edwards, Cramerview; Mrs AM Egan, Bloubergrant; Fay Engelbrecht, Parkhurst; H Glennie, Somerset East; Annabelle Gordon, Hillbrow; Mrs E Greenland, Bloemfontein; Annie Johnson, Somerset West; Bianca Lawrence, Pietermaritzburg; Mrs OM Lee, Risidale; Toni Levin, Bramley; Rose Lloyd, Bathurst; Hannah Lurie, Durban; Jean McAllan, Cathcart; Thelma Michell, Plumstead; Lea Newmark, Onrust River; Mrs H Newnham, Allan Manor; Margaret Poulsom, Saldanha; Jenni Rabinowitz, Constantia; Zuretha Roos, Linden; Linda Sandilands, Krugersdorp North; Emile Shreve, Three Anchor Bay; Ethne Stevens, Kensington, Cape; H Suttner & H Adams, Sea Point; A Walker, Pietermaritzburg; Mrs MF Warren, Bergvliet.